from
Woodstock
up to
Jerusalem

Following the Guideposts
to Healing and Fullness in Christ

Elaine S. Beeler, MA, PCC

Inscript

From Woodstock up to Jerusalem

I dedicate this book to my Mom and Dad, who truly built our family on a firm foundation. However, time and experience changes parents and children get older. So, although my siblings and I had different experiences of our parents, we were all trained by love, discipline, and faith in God. They developed in us the core resiliency to ultimately endure the hardships in our lives and the freedom to enjoy the good times. Thank you, Mom and Dad. Because of you, though I've had many ups and downs in my life, I was able to come back to that core of faith and family which you implanted.

Endure hardship as discipline; God is treating you as his children. For what children are not disciplined by their father?.... Moreover, we have all had human fathers who disciplined us and we respected them for it. How much more should we submit to the Father of spirits and live! ... but God disciplines us for our good, in order that we may share in his holiness.... No discipline seems pleasant at the time, but painful. Later on, however, it produces a harvest of righteousness and peace for those who have been trained by it.

Hebrews 12:7,9,11

Contents

Introduction

Setting the Stage Before It Begins

Not long ago, the Lord told *me,* **"I am taking you out of the marketplace and into my provision."** That was when I began my journey deeper into the ministry of the Word to others through healing and prayer. Specifically, the change meant that I would leave behind the hours, requirements, and income of my Christian professional clinical counseling practice. At about the same time, I felt led to share the amazing journey of healing and wholeness the Lord took me on over a six-year span.

I had been reading the story of David in the cave at En-Gedi, where he defeats Saul with his righteousness alone. ^{1 Samuel 24} Then, the Lord prepared me to walk into this new ministry with these words (the first of many listening prayers I will share). In this word, He speaks to all of His children who are listening:

I gave you this story this morning for a reason. I want you to place your burdens squarely upon me. When I deliver the "enemy" into your hand, do not respond in the flesh! But listen intently for me to speak a word that will fell even the tallest timbers of Lebanon without the aid of man. Let the weight of My Glory fall on you and reveal grace and mercy to the powerful and vengeful. Yes, they will see the glory I have given you in your heart of forgiveness! No more nights of hatred in the battle for my Glory to be the light that blinds the eyes of My enemies.

Feel the Glory in the stillness, the light, the thick air of My Breath. Ask and you shall receive. I (the Lord) ask for the redemption of your world, for the souls of your children to be made whole in the Unity of our Body, one in Adonai, in Me, Yeshua, in Elohim.

I have never been a writer before, nor have I been in the position of shepherdess or pastor within the church. I am a counselor and, as a Christian, have always worked in a ministerial setting. I was not, however, seeking a "writing assignment." But here I was, spending time with the Lord and His word. And with such words as the above pouring out, I knew I was being prepared for the near future.

Before the Journey to Israel and Beyond

Isaiah 35:8
And a highway will be there;
it will be called the Way of Holiness;
it will be for those who walk on that Way.
The unclean will not journey on it;
wicked fools will not go about on it.

The Theme
This scripture became the theme for this book, a theme that the Lord expanded to include Jeremiah 31:21, below. In plain English, the theme of From Woodstock Up to Jerusalem is Learning to Walk in The Way of Holiness *for His Name's Sake*. In the book of Romans, we see the gospel of Christ defined as *the Roman Road*. It is also called the *Road*

to Righteousness. It encompasses everything we experience in our Christian lives, from the fleshly existence in sin, to our salvation and sanctification, to grasping His absolute sovereignty and our life of service. It is as ancient as our faith and yet as fresh as every testimony of faith written since Abraham came on the scene. Each step of that road is different and yet has been repeated and recognized for thousands of years.

Adding anything new to these guideposts that God revealed to me would mean going against His trust and purpose, as described in Ezekiel 36—just before the promise of the new covenant and our invitation into the House of Israel became a reality:

> [22] This is what the Lord GOD says: It is *not for your sake that I will act*, O house of Israel, **but for My holy name**, which you profaned among the nations to which you went. [23] **I will show the holiness of My great name, which has been profaned among the nations**—the name you have profaned among them. Then the nations will know that I am the LORD, declares the Lord GOD, **when I show My holiness in you** before their eyes.

It is for HIS NAME'S SAKE, the restoration of HIS HOLINESS in us, that these guideposts have been written to show His people how to return to the place of honoring GOD through living a transformed life.

Before beginning our journey to Israel, I spent an afternoon in quiet contemplation at our ministry center. There, I was able to soak in the presence and shalom of the Father. I felt I was to write this message to all who would journey with our group in Spirit and in truth and all who read these words; then, deep within, I heard the still, small voice of my Lord:

Let all here know that we who go to Israel (on the journey up to Jerusalem) will bear the gift of the Fa-

ther's Holy Spirit presence. As His holy anointing oil, He will pour the gift into the ministry of the Word. Its weight is so precious and holy; it is heavy, and we are beasts of burden to that land of Israel. Our baskets cannot begin to contain His gifts to all His children.

There are 10 guideposts I will give you on your journey as you return, my new "virgin nation of Israel."

The reference for this rhema Word was Jeremiah 31:21. It reads:

Set up road signs; put up guideposts.
Take note of the highway, the road that you take.
Return, O Virgin Israel, return to your towns.

These guideposts that Jeremiah wrote about are meant for YOU—no matter who you are. If you've picked up this book, whether out of curiosity because you missed Woodstock and once believed hippies had found the perfect alternative lifestyle (spoiler: it's not Marxism!) or because you're a sincere follower of the faith who feels stuck on your spiritual journey, these guideposts are here to help. Each chapter is different but connected to one another because we all will experience and learn about these issues and spiritual disciplines as we mature in life:

- Being born into the New Covenant of Christ;
- Learning how to live a sacrificial life;
- Experiencing Healing in the course of our growth;
- Knowing why and how we must know Righteousness, and,
- Why Suffering is inevitable.

That's just a start; there are five more. But first, I want to explain a little bit about who I am and why this book was birthed through my experience.

Jeremiah 21:31 caught my attention two years ago as a clinical therapist who was pressing into healing and prayer. Oftentimes, I was busy with writing and directing others on the spiritual paths that would guide them to a whole, vibrant, intimate relationship with the Lord. So, when I read Jeremiah 31:21, it felt like a special charge to me, although at the time, I never knew I would be actually going to Israel. It was a distant dream. I did know that we are on that spiritual journey already as part of the grafted-in nation of our Lord. I also believe that we are meant to return one day in our glorified bodies when He comes to Jerusalem to reign in glory. Nonetheless, like many, a burning desire to see my someday homeland stirred within me. I felt I had to know "The Way" there, as I wrote in the margin of my Bible, "Now, how do we set up the guideposts for the return?"

Going Up to Jerusalem

Many Christians today still ask why we should care about Jerusalem. Why pray for her peace? Who really cares? After all, we are Christians now, right? The Jews had their chance and missed it, failed to recognize their Messiah, and, in fact, crucified Him. So why bother with the Old Testament and all that ancient history?

These arguments have been answered very clearly by the Apostle Paul in Romans 9, 10, 11. I touch upon it in Guidepost two, but that is not my purpose here. I simply want to say that my Savior, Jesus, was a Jew. Everything He said and did to give us victory over sin and death was done as a Jew, shaped by His Hebrew culture and deeply devoted to His people. He longed to protect them, like a mother hen gathering her chicks, and He willingly died as a Jew on a Roman cross. Through His sacrifice, He made it possible for us to have the closest, most intimate relationship with the Father.

Compared to the impact of Woodstock on a culture, we can't imagine the impact Jesus in Jerusalem has and will have on this world one day!

I could not write this book if Jesus were not a Jew.

THAT SAID:

I didn't know what "Going Up to Jerusalem" meant until I visited the land itself and put foot to pavement, from the Mediterranean, to the Sea of Galilee, to the Dead Sea and to Jerusalem! It was a reality that exceeded my every expectation. Actually, ascending from the lowest place on earth, the Dead Sea, up to the highest in God's spiritual order changes one's heart, I am convinced, at the cellular level. The nearness of the Lord was palpable, and the atmosphere rarefied by millions of prayers that have ascended like the finest incense to the throne room of our Holy God from antiquity when the temple stood at Shiloh, and later at the Temple Mount of Jerusalem.

Each experience in every site had a special relevance to the idea of "Going Up to Jerusalem." From the countryside to the Old City, from the Mount of Olives to the Pool of Bethesda, and from the Garden of Gethsemane to the ancient steps leading to the Temple—we felt history come alive. Standing at the Wailing Wall and the dark prison pit where Jesus may have been held, our senses were heightened with the anticipation of His return, as if the sound of the shofar was already echoing His message.

"BLESSED BE THE ONE WHO COMES IN THE NAME OF THE LORD! FOR HE IS COMING SOON.

Why did the ancient Hebrew people go up three times a year, and why did they offer their sacrifices in the temple? Simply put, it was to draw near to God. A sacrifice or burnt offering, an "olah" in Hebrew, meant a staircase in the ancient Hebrew—a means of ascending. Going up to Jerusalem became synonymous with going up to God.

Oswald Chambers writes in <u>My Utmost for His Highest</u> (August 3) that "Jerusalem, in the life of our Lord, represents the place where He reached the culmination of His Father's will. Jesus said, 'I do not seek my own will but **the will of the one who sent Me'**" John 5:30 ...He was never deterred from that purpose. 'He steadfastly set His face to go to Jerusalem'" Luke 9:51 "For His Great Name's Sake." Ezek 36

My entire journey to Israel became an experience in the practice of knowing, hearing, and walking in the presence of God, to draw near to God. And yet, when I came to Jerusalem, I was not prepared for the powerful experience of knowing Him even more intimately. He had already revealed himself from the seaport of Netanya to the Sea of Galilee, the Jordan River to Megiddo, En-Gedi, and Qumran. But to this faithful pilgrim, He was a more than faithful, loving Father. He bestowed good, good gifts on this child of His in Jerusalem. I'm sure that it was also a result of the intentionality of the journey, along with the focus and the days of intense prayer I spent while in Jerusalem. But add the enhancement of the actual historic place, and my cup was overflowing!

'Going Up' is what the Lord requires of us, wherever we live, in whatever nation or period of time we live. It is wisdom and obedience to "draw near to God and He will draw near to you." James 4:8 The consequences for those who do not "go up" are clear:

> 16Then it will come about that any who are left of all the nations that went against Jerusalem will go up from year to year to worship the King, the LORD of hosts, and to celebrate the Feast of Booths. 17<u>And it will be that whichever of the families of the earth does not go up to Jerusalem to worship the King, the LORD of hosts, there will be no rain on them.</u> Zechariah 14:16-17

In this scripture, I feel the urgency of this journey we are on and the passion of the Lord for His Hebrew and grafted-in nation as well as His land of Israel. I also hear a warning that if we do not go, there will be a drought of living, spiritual, life-giving water! Do any of us have any choice but to advance in the faith?

Again, Oswald Chambers writes: "The greatest thing for us to remember is that we go up to Jerusalem to fulfill God's purpose, not our own ... In the Christian life, we have no goals of our own ... **'You did not choose Me, but I chose you...' (John 15:16)** "[1]

This writing about the Guideposts will mark the road for the "return of virgin Israel on her way to her own towns." Father God is calling each of us 'Up to Jerusalem.' Although the order of our steps will differ from one another as, spiritually and experientially, we come into our "own" towns, we must go. Sometimes, it will be a lonely journey without our companions in the faith. But we must go on as we learn to trust in the breath and the voice of our Lord, who guides us.

The same day that He stirred my heart to listen for these guideposts before flying to Tel Aviv, He gave me the first guidepost. It was amazing to experience these guideposts on my personal journey to Israel and to Jerusalem. More than an experience, the Father inscribed them indelibly in my spirit and soul. In telling the story of my journey and the impact of these lessons on my life, past and present, I now make them a gift to others who may have occasion to read this. It is my goal and my prayer that the impact of the eternal truths He teaches us here will inspire each traveler on this journey with amazement and delight in the Lord of Hosts!

---

1   My Utmost for His Highest; August 3.

About Listening Prayer

I would like to try to explain the genesis of much of what follows. These ten guideposts have been birthed out of what I consider to be my most intimate dialogue and guidance from the Father. An understanding of my identity in Christ and the ability to enter into this intimacy laid the groundwork for these writings. Although I am not a theologian, I do believe all the scripture is true and meant to be our ultimate guide. Therefore, I first seek guidance in the word regarding all I write. I also believe, however, that the Spirit is pouring himself out in this later day, just as the prophets foretold: *"I will pour out my Spirit on all people. Your sons and your daughters will prophesy..."* [Joel 2:28] The Father is anxious to speak to us today, and I am anxious to hear His voice!

All my life as a Christian, I had learned to pray and then be still and listen for His word. The Father frequently led me to the "perfect" scripture in His word that spoke to me or my needs in amazing ways. So, in this attitude of trust, I learned some years ago, at a "Radically Undone" conference, that I could listen to and write what the Father's Spirit spoke into my heart and mind. Doing this is what I and others refer to as *listening prayer*.[2] Everyone receives from the Father in their own way—visions, music, art, dreams, as well as written forms. All express the Father's heart to us. We learn to recognize His cadence in each, and sharing these prayer responses in a group

---

2   Listening prayer is primarily personal encouragement a believer receives from God. It is not to be equated in any way with the sacred Words written by God's scribes and canonized long ago. It is very personal because it is delivered to one's spirit. What I received from the Holy Spirit, for example, about being washed by the tears of the Father, is metaphorical and should not be interpreted as theological truth. If we did that, it would nullify the truth of the Word that we are washed by the blood of Christ.

helps to validate and clarify what the Lord is saying to us, as well as to eliminate our flesh or the attempts of the enemy to penetrate this Holy ground.

I offer to you what the Father revealed through this prayer time on November 27, 2016, because I firmly believe it was to precede these guideposts that He intended to give for all of us who believe.

In prayer, the question on my heart was, "O Lord, show me the way, the guideposts in the desert leading to Jerusalem, and the Mount of your Ascension and your soon return in Glory."

This is the way you must follow. My Way, my truth, my very Life until death is swallowed up. The veil will be removed for all to see and know that I am God. In that hour, the Brilliance of I Am will ignite the hearts of all Believers, and none will lose their way on that path, paved in the shifting desert sands yet never again covered by a single particle of sand.

Picture Me, my Son, running, dancing, rejoicing on that highway until, out of breath, He stops to embrace every person, creature, plant, tree, flower –sprung up alongside those many wells of water, they line the way, they are Living water. Because millions have run at last to this highway to climb up on it and their feet, wet with Springs of life, have saturated the beautiful land. We rejoice with you (the church!) in unbegotten LOVE, at last united with the millions who keep My divided flame alive in their hearts.

This will be a time of unrequited Joy; no heart can bear the fullness of it. But many hearts, lit by my flame, can unite together in a LOVE so much greater than I, your Father and Creator, can express in words to you.

I need your heart now!! Surrender it to me, and my

unfathomable gratitude for such a gift will ignite wild-fires of love. MY LOVE, which will never be extin-guished again!

Love IS fire, IS light, IS water and Life, IS truly un-stoppable, and you will be prepared to receive it fully and contain it as you extend it to all those whom you touch.

Had you not trudged the desert, fought the wild tigers in thirst and famine of soul with broken heart and wounded minds to reach the High Road now paved in My desert—had you not...you could not contain the Power of my Love I desire to now pour into you. Joyfully embrace your freedom in Love, I AM now.

Abba

My Thanks

My deepest gratitude must go, of course, to my husband, Dale, who supports me and sustains me in all that I imagine, attempt, or actually do! Thank you, dear life partner, who has seen and experienced the best of times and the worst. I thank my children as well, who, whether they knew it or not, were always present with me as I worked out the testimonies of this book; I want to honor them now as they pursue their own paths upward, always up!

I want to pour out my thanks and deepest gratitude to all of my prayer partners who have journeyed with me in the last few years, including the Throne Room Brigade and the Princess Warriors, especially Erin, Matt, Jamie, Betty, Ragan, Amber and Jodi from the DLC, my dear friends Jessa, Dianne, and Becky and many others. I love you all dearly, and I know your prayers have constantly uplifted, protected, and directed me.

Guidepost I

The New Covenant

In my spirit, I sensed the Lord saying:

The first guidepost is my New Covenant, and you have received Me in your heart and mind already. You know my Word, my law spoken into you by the Son, my firstborn.

Then immediately, this scripture fell to hand: Jeremiah 31:33-34:

[33]"But this is the covenant which I will make with the house of Israel after those days," declares the LORD, "I will put My law within them and on their heart I will write it; and I will be their God, and they shall be My people. [34]They will not teach again, each man his neighbor and each man his brother, saying, 'Know the LORD,' for they will all know Me, from the least of them to the greatest of them," declares the LORD, "for I will forgive their iniquity, and their sin I will remember no more."…

And His spirit whispered in my heart:

Treasure these words and shelter them from the enemy (of your souls). My heart is tender towards you, and I know my disciples. I see those who have submitted hearts and minds. I rejoice because I can breathe my truth, and it registers with ease. It is not a struggle to understand and divide the Word. This is your first guidepost.

Abba Daddy

It made perfect sense to me that the first guidepost that I was given was this: we are welcomed fully into the family of Christ and into the new covenant by what Jesus himself described as being born again. He clearly told Nicodemus:

> Jesus replied, "Very truly I tell you, no one can see the kingdom of God unless they are born again. "
> [4]"How can someone be born when they are old?" Nicodemus asked. "Surely they cannot enter a second time into their mother's womb to be born!"
> [5]Jesus answered, "Very truly I tell you, no one can enter the kingdom of God unless they are born of water and the Spirit. [6]Flesh gives birth to flesh, but the Spirit gives birth to spirit. [7]You should not be surprised at my saying, 'You must be born again.' [8]The wind blows wherever it pleases. You hear its sound, but you cannot tell where it comes from or where it is going. So it is with everyone born of the Spirit." John 3:3-8

And so, with these haunting words from Jesus, the mystery begins...

My Testimony: Woodstock Nation to Child of God

Almost nothing in our culture of music, drugs, freedom to Individualize, and the desire to root up and throw out the traditions of our parents, spoke to my generation like the experience and the ideology of "Woodstock Nation." It was no doubt the plan of the enemy of my soul to lure me to that event and make it a powerful statement of my identity at the age of 18. The plan worked. It was August 15, 1969, and there at Yasgur's farm, I reveled with many others in a boundless and seemingly endless mass of unwashed and unkempt hippies for 4 days of intoxicating music, drugs, and promiscuity. I was so sold on the lie I told a reporter there taping the medivac removal of a young person with a broken leg: "You shouldn't focus on that! That's not the news. Can't you see the beauty of what's happening around you? That's the news!" Oddly enough, I don't think my statement was ever broadcast. Possibly, the way that I arrived at Woodstock is the best part of my story. Technically, I arrived in an ice cream truck with a friend because we had jobs in New Jersey driving an ice cream route! He suggested the trip and sold the company on the idea that it might even be profitable. Of course, like everyone, we were stuck in hours of traffic jams, and the festival was sold out before we reached the gate. He left me there and beat his way back for more ice cream because the organizers were so desperate for food. The primary chuck wagon was provided by the "Pig Farm" commune, which traveled with the Grateful Dead. Not exactly a professional outfit ready for the task of feeding 200,000 hungry hippies. My friend and I reconnected later, although the ice cream was no more.

But when did that journey, my odyssey "Up to Woodstock" really begin? It was likely part of my flight from the painful realities of my life, beginning with the death of my sister, an especially horrible suicide because she was pregnant at the time. It was followed by the death of my father, a beloved local pediatrician, to cancer a year later. Those events shattered a 1950s Ozzie and Harriet-like family and cast me adrift at the age of 14 into depression and alcohol (also my mother's escape route) as well as anger and rebellion against the "establishment." The mid-sixties offered me lots of ways to protest; the civil rights movement and the Vietnam War ignited my anger and depressed fury into action as I took every bus the local Unitarian church offered to various marches. A caveat here is important: I still do not pass judgment on the righteousness or lack thereof regarding the war, and I would not undo what the civil rights movement accomplished. But as a teenager of 14-17, I really was ignorant of so much and cared more about "anti-disestablishmentarianism," our BIG word, than the war or civil rights.

My moral disintegration was quick and easy as drugs entered the scene, and I prided myself on being the first at my high school to get high on marijuana. However, with the stain of suicide/infanticide on my family's soul and my own depression growing steadily as I fed it with drugs, alcohol, and sex, a break was coming. In the strange way our psyches work, I somehow "unconsciously" chose the anniversary of my sister's suicide to attempt suicide myself for the first time in my life. Obviously, it failed, but I did manage to break my mother's fragile heart all over again. She responded with a trip to the emergency room and somehow connected me with a psychiatrist. Medications were not in vogue at that time, but the psychiatrist told me I was angry at my mother, and that seemed to be the reason for my actions. A young woman of 16 rarely has insight into these things, so I scoffed at his suggestion and went on with my life. But of course, he was right, and I was angry! I was angry at the world and everyone in it. Anger was giving me the energy to fuel my addictions and every rebellious action I took at that time, from skipping school to marching in war protests in D.C. That little trip, by the way, was sponsored by a local church that was very pro-social justice and not opposed to taking a couple of teenagers across the country on flimsy, forged permission slips.

Pause: A Clinical Diagnostic Perspective

Now, the evidence that I was behaving as a manic-depressive began to mount. Did I ever tell this "doctor of the mind" that my mother and uncle had "rescued" me from a slovenly apartment where I was holed up with my boyfriend, indulging in drugs, alcohol, and sex? And then I heard that word "slut" from my mother for the first time? I don't think I would have told the psychiatrist this because I was indeed filled with shame at that point. I knew that the complete sense of worthlessness I felt was my subconscious reason for the suicide attempt. I thank God I was incompetent and cowardly and lived through that, as well as the other two times much later in life.

But the question must be asked. Were my suicidal actions the result of a genetically inherited tendency towards mania and depression (later given the description of bipolar disorder)? Or were they the result of the deep feelings of shame, abandonment, hopelessness, and self-loathing because of the losses in my life, especially the suicide of my sister?

Familial Traits:

There is strong evidence that suicidal ideation and action can be linked to inherited psychiatric illnesses. Obviously, major depression and bipolar depression are the most commonly identified.

My family, which to outsiders appeared highly functioning, also had an unhealthy tendency toward alcohol abuse. On the other hand, there was a great deal of fun: boating of all sorts and family singing when reunions occurred. It would be impossible in retrospect to identify the mania of bipolar disorder in my parents, but my observation of my sister who committed suicide was that her love of theatre, dance, singing, and generally being "the life of the party" could have been typical manic behavior.

Spiritual Warfare:

The point must be made briefly, and explained in more detail later, that whatever the external circumstances were in my family and culture, some things had wounded my spirit. The enemy of our souls, who "prowls about looking for someone to devour" (1 Pet 5:8), found me unprotected and wide open and attacked. I am so very thankful that he has lost the battle in my life, and Jesus has won me, heart, mind, soul, spirit, and body!!

Back to My Story: 1969 The Year of Woodstock and Following

I began seeking the light when, by the age of 17, I was a very depressed, angry, and lost young hippie. I graduated from high school with no idea what to do, so I enrolled in the state university. The summer before, a beautiful young man with a spiritual bent stole my heart and talked about "love, peace, and enlightenment" without drugs. I joined his cult and gave the Theosophical movement in Daytona Beach a try, only to find it vacuous, powerless, and meaningless. Back home the next summer, I tried another cult: the Maharishi Mahesh Yogi came to Chicago, and I was discipled into the Transcendental Meditation movement, which essentially made me a Buddhist. I was serious enough in my seeking that I changed colleges and attended the College of Wooster, Ohio, for about a year because it was closer to my boyfriend and because it actually offered a major in Indian (Eastern) Studies. I dutifully read the Bhagavad Gita and much ancient Indian poetry at that time.

Again, although I could meditate and remove myself from consciousness, not a single bit of enlightened thinking or behavior ever entered my life for those two years.[3] All

---

3   An important aside must be mentioned here. Sadly, this type of

I gained was a deeper desire for more escape in the ways I already knew: sex, drugs, and rock'n'roll. I also found a guy who wanted to marry me, seemed to love me, and would take me off my mother's hands. We fell in love just in the nick of time. I was preparing to hitchhike to California with my dog, L.A. Trucker, and hang out with the editor of the L.A. underground paper. He had invited me after we met at the Atlanta Pop Festival. Knowing someone for three days and hitchhiking thousands of miles to live with them made perfect sense to me then. I am so grateful to God for His timing, which moved me in a completely different direction!

Somehow, I avoided pregnancy until, at the age of 19 and engaged, I did conceive. Still in college, it was no debate as we accepted the money from a wealthy friend and flew off to New York for a "legal abortion," one which left me septic and feverish for days. Such amazing delusion seems hard to conceive of, but I was a ready and available vessel for the enemy's plan to destroy a culture of moral, righteous, hard-working Americans who, although they had their faults, had survived the Second World War. The enemy had his plan to devour many of us children of the 60s in a single generation. I agreed with it every step of the way.

It was a rapid transition. I was deluded with romantic love that took me from "Woodstock Nation" in 1969—believing that all you need is love and the right kind of groovy high—to married and living in a small college town in Ohio. It was there that God answered the desperate cries of my

---

meditation has now been repackaged by some within the Schools of Kingdom ministry movement around the church at large and is being called "Contemplative Prayer.." It is not Christian Contemplative prayer in any sense that we have been taught over the centuries. Christian contemplation is to focus on words of truth found in scripture and allow them to inform our thoughts and emotions and to enrich our own spirits. It should never lead to a vacuous nothingness, or worse, allow the entrance of "spirit guides.."

heart that emanated out of my pain over the years: "God, if you ARE real, Show Me!" And there, I met a group of "Jesus Freaks" and a wonderful mentoring Episcopalian priest who led me to the cross shortly after I was married. My husband seemed to have come to believe, too, and all was well in our little world for a while.

The Gift of the Holy Spirit

As a new believer at the age of 20, I received the Holy Spirit with the gift of tongues. That night, I experienced a vivid dream in which I was standing on a bridge and saw a white dove come down and rest on my shoulder. That night was filled with waking and sleeping worship. Since then, I have almost never doubted the reality of His presence in my life. Almost immediately, I noticed that I could no longer meditate using the mantra word given to me as an initiate in Transcendental Meditation. That evil portal was permanently closed. Even so, it took many years before I began to die to self in such a way that His presence could begin to guide me. All of us in that group retained our somewhat unconventional "hippie" style of dress and other cultural emblems. We were the "Jesus Freaks," although we spoke our faith out strongly, few would have noticed the beginnings of changes in our lifestyle. But in His Holy Spirit, I experienced the gift of faith that was unrelenting. God began a massive overhaul of my character, which was so riddled with flaws that it's taken years. In fact, it will never be finished until I leave this mortal coil.

Now, 50 years later, after many years of falling, backward steps, and side trails, and then many years of breaking free, restoration, and inner healing through an inevitable divorce, the tragic loss of my young son, remarriage, and the challenges of raising two children while working as a social worker and counselor in ministry, we arrive here at the incredible, inspiring, and blessed privilege to go "Up to Jerusalem," becoming a part of the grafted-in nation of the children of God through Christ Jesus my Lord. I have found what I was searching for in my deluded youth! Woodstock Nation doesn't begin to imitate the truth of a Nation of Believers in Yeshua!

Whew. Deep Breath. Back to our lesson and journey...

Present-Day Journey to Israel: The Mustard Seed Plan

As this journey to the Holy Land was being conceived, something special was birthed. Our group leader had an inspiration from the Lord to give us mustard seeds to carry with us. She put them in a tiny bottle with a cork and a cord so we could wear them around our necks. Then, we were each to plant those seeds in various places as He led, with the prayers and intentions of our hearts.

This is how the Lord began to show me, during our time in Israel, the significance of this first guidepost, the New Covenant, for His plans and purposes there.

When we came to Netanya, I shared an evening of prayer with friends. There, I felt the strong call from God to pray for His emerging Messianic Priesthood, those who will lead His new covenant church in Israel and around the world. I went out later to plant a mustard seed near the sea and found that the cork would not come out of my tiny bottle. In fact, it had broken off. I knew then that I needed to plant all my seeds together in that garden spot because, at that moment, they represented the seeds of His Messianic promise to return and rule the nations. Like the root of Jesse (*And again, Isaiah says, "The **Root of Jesse** will spring up, one who will arise to rule over the nations; in him the Gentiles will hope"* (Rom 15:12)), it is a promise to birth the new covenant within all believers in this new age, but especially in His New

Priesthood. The law is now being written on the hearts of Jewish believers in Yeshua. And now they fulfill the Father's deepest longing for a pure and undefiled priestly nation. They are not the only ones who will serve, but they bring such joy to the Father's heart! I have carried this prayer of intercession with me throughout Israel and ever since. Why? Because it was God's heart and His revealed desire or prayer burden for me to do so.

The Holy Spirit and the Covenant

The New Covenant was birthed in us, the believers in Yeshua, as He promised it would be with His death, resurrection, and gift of the Holy Spirit. It is essential that we know this truth, described by the Lord in John: 16-5-15, before going on in this study. Without the foundational knowledge that "all that belongs to the Father is mine (the Lord's); (and) That is why I (the Lord) said the Spirit will take from what is mine and make it known to you"(John 16:15), none of what follows will make one iota of sense.

The apostle Paul, at a much later date, following Pentecost, writes in 1 Corinthians 2:9-10, "However as it is written: 'No eye has seen, no hear has heard, no mind has conceived what God has prepared for those who love him' but God has revealed it to us by his Spirit." Then, the explanation of this mystery follows

[10] The Spirit searches all things, even the deep things of God. [11] For who knows a person's thoughts except their own spirit within them? In the same way no one knows the thoughts of God except the Spirit of God. [12] What we have received is not the spirit of the world, but the Spirit who is from God, so that we may understand what God has freely given us. [13] This is what we speak, not in words taught us by human wisdom but in words taught by the Spirit, explaining spiritual realities with

Spirit-taught words.[b] [14] The person without the Spirit does not accept the things that come from the Spirit of God but considers them foolishness, and cannot understand them because they are discerned only through the Spirit. [15] The person with the Spirit makes judgments about all things, but such a person is not subject to merely human judgments, [16] for,

"Who has known the mind of the Lord
  so as to instruct him?"[c]
But we have the mind of Christ. 1 Cor 2:10-16

In this passage, we learn about the amazing ability of the Spirit of God to communicate the will of God to us and within us. Spirit is used 9 times as Paul digs for the words to describe Him: *"The Spirit searches all things, even the deep things of God" (1 Cor* 2:10). How could God hide anything of Himself from His Spirit? He doesn't! The point Paul is making is to contrast the Holy Spirit with the human spirit and point out how limited we are. Our spirits know all things about ourselves, yet we are often out of touch with that knowledge; we seem to be guarded, cut off, or protected from awareness. This brings on all kinds of problems, illnesses, and emotional dysfunction. But God has never lost touch with any of His thoughts and plans. He knows them all and knows us ALL in detail.

Now think about how we have received God's own Spirit so that we may *"freely understand what God Has freely given us" (verse 12).* What is this? All the promises of the gospel, yes, and the ability to UNDERSTAND. We now have the key to greater self-awareness and the knowledge of how we fail to allow God access to us. Now, if we ask God for wisdom, He gives it; for Greater Love, we receive it; for the power to transform our minds and be more Christlike in character, He gladly shows us all things we need to repent of and renounce in that process. Verses 13-14 describe how the Spirit teaches him (Paul) to teach spiritual truths that can only be discerned by the spiritual man (the man who has received the Holy Spirit). Then says the apostle, the spiritual man, "makes judgments about all things [things not people], *but he himself is not subject to any man's judgment: For who has known the mind of the Lord that he may instruct him?" But we have THE MIND OF CHRIST"* (verses 15-16).

What does having the mind of Christ mean? This plainly says we can understand what God is thinking and saying and how He wants us to live, judge the things about us, and proceed. That's a scary, huge responsibility! Are we able to step into this responsibility in great humility? Because God has chosen the foolish things of this world (YOU and I), to shame the wise, the weak to shame the strong, the lowly and the despised things, and the *"things that are not, to nullify the things that are, so that no one may boast before him."* 1 Cor 1:27-28

Caution

It really isn't quite that simple, however. To "have the mind of Christ" is a gift of enlightenment that comes to the believer somewhat rarely at first, in my far-less-than-a-super-saint experience. The process of emptying oneself of all soulish desires, thoughts, attitudes, and emotions, as well as eliminating the oppression that keeps us stuck in this "worldly" mindset, is, well, a process we call *sanctification*. There seem to be flashes of insight given to the humble believer and, in my experience, seasons of clarity, followed sometimes by years of more wandering in the desert of my mind. As one matures, that position or placement with Christ "at the Father's right hand" seems to increase with more confidence and security. And "having the Mind of Christ" seems more a reality as one walks in confidence and freedom in Christ. "Having the Mind of Christ" also requires that we have daily taken "every thought captive and made it obedient to him" (2 Cor. 10:5). We are the ones who hold onto arguments and pretensions that set us up to be in opposition to the knowledge of God. This is the hard work, the demolition work, that we must do as we daily die to self, in concert with the gifts we have been given: "His divine power has given us everything we need for life and godliness through our knowledge of him... so that through them you may participate in the divine nature." 2 Pet 1:3-4

The Mind of Christ and The New Covenant

Recall the words of Jeremiah 31: 33-34:

33"But this is the covenant which I will make with the house of Israel after those days," declares the LORD, "I will put My law within them and on their heart I will write it; and I will be their God, and they shall be My people. 34They will not teach again, each man his neighbor and each man his brother, saying, 'Know the LORD,' for they will all know Me, from the least of them to the greatest of them," declares the LORD, "for I will forgive their iniquity, and their sin I will remember no more."...

Because we have received the baptism of the Holy Spirit, we also have *the* mind of Christ, which refers back to Jer. 31:33, and we have entered the new covenant relationship. We now have the promises of our Lord and Savior, Yeshua; because of His sacrificial offering on the cross, our iniquity is forgiven, and our sin is no longer remembered. But we must recognize and remember that God made this promise to His Holy Nation, the people of Israel, those He allowed to be led out of slavery through the desert and to be settled in their own nation. In 2 Corinthians 3: 14-18, we are told that "whenever anyone turns to the Lord, the veil is taken away," but for now, most of the Jewish nation remains veiled like Moses. However, we, His Gentile people, have been grafted in, and we are given eyes to see! That is why we rejoice in the harvest now taking place in Israel, as more and more of the people of God's First covenant are receiving the Spirit and accepting Christ. The spirit of stupor is being removed from Israel! Paul wrote in Romans 11:12:

> If their transgression means riches for the world, and their loss means riches for the Gentiles, how much greater riches will their fullness bring!

My Story: The Jordan River Baptism

While in Israel, I made a covenant to become a part of the Bride of Christ at my baptism in the Jordan River. I was astonished at God's presence as I waited to enter the Jordan. His Spirit fell over me in waves of joy, awe, and terror, with many tears at the statement I was making with my renewed covenant. I wondered at this greater measure of joy that was inundating me! It was so much more than I had experienced as a new believer. I did not see the white dove again, but there were two swans courting and then mating nearby! What an incredible symbol for the married couples in our group. Many of them covenanted with their spouses during their baptism with beautiful words of recommitment. But there were many of us there, like me, without the honor of a spouse present.

I was reminded then that, as part of the Bride of Christ, I can come to the wedding banquet because others who were invited before me did not come (Matthew 22:3 and 8) and that I can keep my oil full and my lamp lit for the coming of the Groom only by the power and presence of the Holy Spirit (Matt 25:10). Even better than that, I am blessed to have His spiritual gift of unconditional love rooted and growing within me. He sustains me as I learn to love my husband and others for exactly who they are now, in this moment. Without a doubt, in my right-now life, it is the Father's sovereign intention that I learn His character trait of unconditional love. And, yes, through the trials of marriage and raising children who are not yet seeking to walk in His ways, I am learning.

He also impressed me with this truth, even more to the point:

> "He who unites himself with the Lord is one with him in spirit. Your body is a temple of the Holy Spirit, who is in you, whom you have received from God. You are not your own; you were bought at a price. So honor God with your body." 1 Cor. 6: 17; 19-20

In my baptism of the "body," soul, and spirit in the Jordan River, I honored my Lord and became His as much as I could imagine in this life. It was beautiful, exciting, unnerving, and overwhelming for one not normally moved to tears and public displays of emotion. But it is complete, and I will honor this covenant until I meet my Savior and Bridegroom face to face.

Our Spiritual Key for the Journey: Entering the New Covenant

Know that you have become the Covenantal Bride of Christ, and light your lamps now. Keep them filled by the power and the Presence of the Holy Spirit, and never let that light go out once you have received it! Welcome the gift of unrelenting faith and the trials that build the character of Christ within you. And you will go into the wedding banquet with Him when the Bridegroom arrives, before the door is shut! Matt 25:10

Listening Prayer

In a time of prayer six months before I left for Israel, I began to focus on these scriptures:

- "Thy kingdom come."
- "The kingdom of God is within you; it will not come with your careful observation."
- "For the son of man in His day will be like the lightning which flashes and lights up the sky from one end to the other."

I then wrote the following impressions from the Spirit:

In all these ways, I am telling you I am here, and my Spirit is the kingdom. My Spirit will grow and grow within you and all the church until it ignites in spontaneous combustion, and I come in my Glory. I do not need my Bride to come up to me, but I want her!! And so, I patiently wait...but not forever. Dress diligently in gowns of glowing light daily and put on the full armor of my Spirit against the onslaught of evil. Do not be taken by surprise. Be ready to give the testimony I have given you by your life. Let my Words filler this life you live and expose the TRUTH of my walk in you from the beginning. Nothing is wasted in the secret places where Satan worked what he did for evil—I have already planned for good, the Father God's Glory!!

Those who you fear have suffered needlessly; yes, even they will receive my greatest glory within them. Fear not what must come. It must be so in chaos and great loss because, from the beginning, my Elohim (Spirit) has yearned to be wed. Wed to me in simplicity and purity through you.

Invite all you meet to drink of this cup I offer, the bitterness of salt water, the sweetness of wine in my blood together are the source of life. [I pondered the bitterness of salt, its necessity to life and in the body, to homeostasis].

This is a mystery indeed. How the son of man transcended the body of flesh in the presence of Holy Light, filled and illuminated and passing through the veil of this world. Learn "the power of His resurrection and the fellowship of His suffering" so that You, my children, belong to my kingdom. And my coming will ignite your spiritual transformation. Your 'set point' must be high. Prepare – prepare... Amen

Reflections

Out of Bondage, Exile and Slavery:

Write out your own testimony of bondage, or "slavery" and "exile." Share it with a friend and begin to prepare yourself to share with others as God calls. We are asked to always be prepared to give an answer for the hope that we have in Christ. As you articulate that experience over and over in your own words, you give power to the Testimony of Christ.

The New Covenant:

As a fully grafted-in child of God, have you experienced:

1. an altered and reverential awe of the God of Abraham, Isaac, and Jacob
2. greater love for the Jewish people and Israel
3. a desire to pray for their ultimate redemption
4. awareness that you may be called to make them jealous of the Love of Christ in you.

The Holy Spirit:

1. Have you actively asked for or sought the gift of the Holy Spirit?
2. If you have, can you identify ways in which He has begun to alter your life and direct you in the process of sanctification? (The Gift of tongues is not necessary to life in the Spirit).
3. Have you been able to accept your exalted and humble position as a part of the Bride of Christ?
4. Do you keep your oil filled and your lamp lit to await His return?

Guidepost II

Sacrifice

My Glory comes in the sacrificial death of my only Son. A pain so deep, a wellspring eternal of my tears necessary to wash the sins of my beloved children from their souls so we could be reunited once more, now pours forth. <u>This is everything a Father has to give.</u>

When one walks in faith through that valley, trusting my Son, the wellspring of tears that wash away sin is renewed. Because in faith met with sacrifice, I birth mercy, grace, all compassion, and forgiveness. Nothing evil can stand before such a heart as this.

April 5, 2017

Why is Sacrifice the second Guidepost? I believe that the Lord needed to emphasize sacrifice to us immediately, because without the sacrifice of Christ, the New Covenant would be null and void. Most of us understand that. But do we know and accept that we, too, will be called to live a sacrificial life if we are to one day be fully sanctified by Christ in God's power and receive the Crown of Righteousness as His very own child?

The Journey to Israel

On the evening of April 28, 2017, after a safe crossing and landing in Tel Aviv, we drove to our hotel in Netanya by the beautiful Mediterranean Sea. It was lovely to walk by the seashore and swim in its crystalline waters while taking time to digest all that I had read and seen on our journey over the Atlantic and the continent of Europe.

Two things stood out to me from the flight. We were blessed to share the cabin with many orthodox, observant Jews and see them praying Shabbat prayers the morning of our arrival. Their devotion and persistence to dress appropriately and stand while reciting their prayers were undeterred by the requests to sit and fasten seatbelts. I saw at least three men fasten the tefillin or phylacteries upon their foreheads in this process and thought of the first guidepost I had been impressed with: "I will put my law in their minds and write it on their hearts." Secondly, here was the clear evidence of the Old Testament covenant before me as these observant men remembered the deliverance of their nation from the bondage of slavery by wearing the scrolls kept in these little black boxes and strapped to their foreheads. Some phylacteries are also worn bound to the arm, a tradition we also witnessed.

It was in the evening, during a time of prayer and worship with friends, that the Spirit impressed upon me to stop and write this word:

My presence in this land is sacrificial, and my people have not and will not enter the Holy of Holies without sacrifice. For you, this is an open door to intercede because brokenness has tied my nation's hands like phylacteries upon the forehead...MY WORD is alive and sears the mind and soul and Spirit of My Life in this nation. Pray without ceasing because My Love is in your heart.

The Interpretation, for me

It came as quite a surprise to me that I was being charged with intercession, probably one among thousands, to call up and forth the soon-to-be rabbinical, priestly leaders of the Messianic Jewish community in Israel and the world. When one begins to pray in obedience, and the words of intercession come out, the Father's heart is revealed, and this was the direction He was pointing me. There are men and women ready to receive the completeness of their faith in Yeshua and prepare to share it with the world. Whatever blocks them from this path in the spirit realm must be removed so that they can fulfill this calling. For these individuals, especially within the conservative culture of Judaism in Israel, it is a tremendous sacrifice to proclaim Yeshua et Hamashiach (Jesus Is the Messiah). They are ostracized and cut off from the rest of the conservative Jewish believers. *"You will be handed over to the local councils and flogged in the synagogues. On account of me..."* Jesus prophesied. Matthew 10:17, Mark 13:9

We remember that long before our Lord came to Earth, Isaiah prophesied that *"the Root of Jesse will spring up, one who will arise to rule over the nations: the Gentiles will hope in him"* (Isaiah 11:10). This is the seed planted before the foundations of the Earth that Paul recognized as our Lord, from whom all our blessings flow. Praise God that we are now witnessing what Paul wrote about his countrymen: *"Whenever anyone turns to the Lord, the veil is taken away!"* The result: the Spirit comes, there is freedom, and *"we who with unveiled faces all reflect the Lord's glory, are being transformed into his likeness with ever-increasing glory, which comes from the Lord, who is the Spirit."* 2 Cor 3:16-18 All because of the ultimate sacrifice, the life of the Lord, given on the cross for the remission of the sins of the world. *"God made him who had no sin to be sin for us, so that in him we might become the righteousness of God."* 2 Cor 5:21 Can we grasp the depth and the riches of the sacrifice of God our Father?

This is everything a Father has to give! And He was given to gain the life of the world!

The Meaning for Us

The larger meaning of sacrifice for all who desire to follow the road back and go "Up to Jerusalem" is rich and runs deep like a vein of solid gold through the ancient Torah and New Testament scriptures. As I studied the word, three Bible stories unfolded for me, and I began to understand the sacred, sovereign, and sacrificial circumstances in my own life. In the gold mine of the scriptures we have been allowed to dig into, we discover much about sacrifice.[4] Abraham laid down the life of Isaac on an altar before God but received the sacrificial offering before the fire was lit. Gen 22 Jephthah made an unholy vow before God; it was not a covenant promise from God, and he actually did sacrifice his own daughter as a burnt offering. Judges 11:30-40 Finally, Hannah made a vow to give her child to the service of the Lord if He would look upon her, remember her, and give her a son. 1 Samuel 1:11 Her vow, however, unlike Jephthah's, became a covenant when God responded YES by breathing life into Hannah's womb to bring forth the Prophet Samuel.

---

4   You may want to read these stories before reading the rest of this chapter.
•Abraham and Isaac, Genesis 22
•Jepthah's daughter, Judges 11:30-40
•Hannah and Samuel, 1 Samuel 1

What Results from Sacrifice?

➢ For the Nation of Israel: Abraham and Isaac

It is evident that the sacrifice of God's one and only Son resulted in life eternal for all who believe. But did life come from the act of sacrifice that Abraham was willing to make? Most emphatically, yes! The angel of the Lord called to Abraham from heaven a second time and said, "I swear by myself, declares the Lord, that because you have done this and have not withheld your son, your only son, I will surely bless you and make your descendants as numerous as the stars in the sky and as the sand on the seashore.... And through your offspring all nations on earth will be blessed, because you have obeyed me." Gen 22:16-18 The scripture assures us that the Jewish nation is a nation of priests who will again bless the world.

> "Although the whole earth is mine, you will be for me a kingdom of priests and a holy nation." Ex 19:6

Add to that the word from Paul we reviewed above concerning the remnant of Israel:

> "... For if their rejection is the reconciliation of the world, what will their acceptance be but life from the dead?... if the root is holy, so are the branches!" Rom. 11:15,16

We are branches grafted in because of Abraham's obedience, which established a nation for the Lord in which we can find our salvation through the promised Messiah, Yeshua! Hallelujah! We pray for and await the eventual redemption of the entire remnant of the Jewish nation as they accept Yeshua as their Messiah.

➢ For Hannah and Samuel

Likewise, we know that Hannah's sacrifice produced the prophet Samuel:

"The Lord was with Samuel as he grew up, and he let none of his <u>words</u> fall to the ground...the Lord continued to appear at Shiloh, and there he revealed himself to Samuel through his <u>word.</u> And <u>Samuel's word</u> came to all Israel." [1 Sam. 3:19-21]

Remember that the word of the prophet is God-breathed and holy, giving life! Just as Jesus was "the Word and the Word was with God and the Word was God... in him was Life!" [John 1:1,4]

The Father also blessed Hannah after her sacrificial release of Samuel. He gave her more children! A whole quiver full. Our God honors us and loves those who enter into a life of sacrifice.

➤ Jephthah the Gileadite and His Daughter

But what are we to do with the troubling story of Jephthah the Gileadite and the sacrifice of his virgin daughter? I have many questions but only a hunch as an answer. Did God actually call Jephthah to make this sacrifice, or was it his own idea? When he crossed Gilead and advanced against the Ammonites, he made a vow to the Lord: "If you give the Ammonites into my hand, whatever comes out of the door of my house to meet me when I return in triumph from the Ammonites will be the Lord's, and I will sacrifice it as a burnt offering." Look back at Judges 11:1 and learn that Jephthah was the son of Gilead and a prostitute. He was driven away and disinherited from the family by the sons of Gilead's wife. Jephthah was known as a "mighty warrior," and when the nation was in need, the elders of Gilead went to get Jephthah from the land where he was exiled. Jephthah was suddenly needed, and they offered to make him head and commander over them if he delivered them from the Ammonites.

Jephthah, as I see him, was a wounded, disinherited, stigmatized man who, in his brokenness, grasped at the opportunity to be redeemed. To ensure his own success, his value, and his worth to others, he made an unholy vow to the Lord to provide an unknown sacrifice of something within his household. His daughter came out of the door to greet him when he returned, fulfilling the condition of his vow. He lost his only daughter. There was no redemption of life as a result of this sacrifice.

Lesson learned: a sacrifice made "to God" that is motivated by selfish interests is no sacrifice at all. Sacrifices made unto God because they are directed by His voice or inspired by His heart lead to life and abundant blessings.

My Testimony

My understanding of sacrifice began when I was 36 and met and married my second husband. At that time, we both were solid Christians who had been hurt by divorce. He had one child, a seven-year-old girl, and I had a son, Blair, who was five. In addition to my loss through divorce, I had many losses early in life, as I described previously. At nineteen, I also lost my first child by my first fiancé to abortion. All before I accepted Christ as my savior at the age of twenty.

During much of my 20s, I failed to mature in my faith and nearly lost my faith completely for a while. Thankfully, Jesus never let go of me. I simply was not ready to let go of the world that my alternative lifestyle "new world" idealism dictated. While living in California near Carmel, I tried the Unitarian Church for a little while and, sadly, found it empty. There is much more to say about that decade, which ended with the birth of my son, a divorce, and my second failed attempt at suicide, but that is for another time.

During the divorce, at the age of 31, I was led by the Lord to return to my home city and begin attending a solid church that was full of the Spirit, as the Charismatic movement was sweeping through mainstream churches everywhere. Suffice it to say, a lot of work by the Holy Spirit through inner healing, "Breaking Free" prayer, and personal counseling, as well as a deepening walk into committed discipleship, prepared me to re-marry at 36 and for what followed shortly after.

Two years after we married, we felt happy and content with our new family and our new home. My son, Blair, was an intelligent and curious child and given as much love as a mother can give. He seemed mature beyond his years. One day, for example, he would not get in the car to go on our errand and seemed entranced with the ground. "What," I exclaimed, "are you doing?" His answer: "Just experiencing the world around me, mother." Where that came from, I have not a clue, although it sounded like his father, who also loved to examine every small thing in detail.

In the fall of 1988, my son, now eight, was struck by a car while crossing the road going to his piano lesson. The traffic had been barricaded due to construction, and I had just let him out of the car, so I witnessed the entire tragedy. We were rushed to the local hospital by ambulance and then medevacked to the regional Children's Hospital downtown. I was in such shock that many details are lost to me, but somehow, I was taken to his bedside. He did not die instantly but held on because of his strong young heart, although later, I would be told that his brain had died immediately. I was reduced to desperate and fervent prayer as I knelt by his bedside for hours. And in the breaking of my heart, this mother's pleas for life for her son did not fall on a cold, distant, uncaring God. Instead, the Father, my Abba, gave me the most precious gift one could imagine in that circumstance, short of a complete and miraculous healing. He opened Heaven to me in a vision so that I could see and hear Blair there with the Lord Jesus. Across a creek, Blair came and stood before me. He then said to me, "Come on, Mom; it's just like Ireland, only greener!" In the background, up on a hill beneath a tree, I could see one man whom I believed to be Jesus with the little children gathered around Him. I tearfully looked into Blair's sweet, whole, healthy, and perfect face as I stood on 'the other side' and said, "I'm sorry, I can't come now; you go on without me, and I will come later." He looked sad yet had a knowing peace about him as he turned back toward Jesus, and the vision faded. His heart stopped beating the next morning, and mine was ripped in two.

Within two weeks of being plunged into this new life of grief and loss, a friend who presided over our local Cincinnati Crisis Pregnancy Center called and asked if I would consider taking the position of Social Worker and Counselor at the center, which had recently opened. She knew of my interest in healing the scars of abortion and providing alternatives because of my own experience and my volunteer work with shepherding homes several years before. She did not know of Blair's death.

However, I already knew that God was stirring my heart to reengage in that work to stem the painful tide of abortions, and He had turned my thoughts and heart in that direction before Blair's death. So, I promised to pray, and within a short time, I felt absolutely certain that here was where God meant for me to pour out all the grace and mercy, healing Love, and forgiveness that He had poured into my life. I briefly struggled with the thought of "so much death and sadness in the lives of these women, how can I deal with it?" but the death of my son, which my enemy, the evil one, had meant to use to devour my life with bitterness and remorse, my Abba Father meant to use in order to breathe life into women who were either contemplating abortion or post-abortive. I said, "Yes."

19 Years Earlier

My first son, whom I lost to abortion, was called Samuel. Not by my choice but by God. He revealed this name to me in a dream when, in my early 30s, I was healed of that loss. Samuel means "Called of God" or "Heard of God." I didn't realize that one day, when the name Samuel was revealed to me, it would so poignantly remind me of Hannah's sacrifice. I sympathize with Hannah's loss, no matter how willingly she gave up her son to God's service. At the time of Blair's death, the message of Samuel's name, "called of God," was brought into sharp focus when I answered yes to the call of God myself. I knew that taking on the difficult assignment at the Crisis Pregnancy Center to address the ravages of abortion in our city would honor the losses of my own two boys. In the face of my losses, I would seek God's will by seeking life in the dark place of the abortion industry.

Because names have been so meaningful to me, I learned that my son Blair's name, by interpreting the meaning of the ancient Hebrew letters Beit, Lamed, and Resh, can mean "teacher of what is most important in the family." I can attest that during their very short lives, these two sons did indeed lead me to God in desperate prayers for life, for them and for the unborn, to be called of God and to learn what is most important in the family of God. What I have learned to value above all is the love of God and the life He gives, the sacrifice of Christ for and in us, and the breath of God, who is the continuous giver of Life:

"As it is written:
'for your sake we face death all day long;
we are considered as sheep to be slaughtered.'

No, in all these things we are more than conquerors through him who loved us. For I am convinced that neither death nor life, neither angels nor demons, neither the present nor the future, nor any powers, neither height nor depth, nor anything else in all of creation will be able to separate us from the love of God that is in Christ Jesus our Lord!" ^{Rom 8:36-39}

What God Did to Help Me Make A Sacrifice

It is not difficult now for me to fathom how God, in His mercy, withheld judgment, forgiving me for my sin of abortion many years before. In giving me that vision of Blair, the absolute personal assurance of life after death, He gave me the grace to also make a sacrifice. What did I sacrifice? I think it was, first of all, the dream of the perfect all-American Christian family. Although it was a blended "second chance" family, to me, it seemed perfect. I had to surrender that pathway to happiness. I also sacrificed "my time" of mourning and sorrow, my "right" to be bitter, angry and self-absorbed. I could have chosen to die by my own means or self-neglect and would have been pitied by others. It was a type of sacrifice to accept the loss and choose to live instead, for others, through the redemptive mission of the pro-life movement. However, the greatest blessing to me of this terrible loss and sacrifice was that I had acquired first-hand experience of what our Abba-Daddy, our Sovereign Father, felt when He lost His only begotten Son. God's incredible deep pain...His loss evokes such compassion in me for His heart and my Savior's journey through life and death that I love them, Father, Son, and Spirit, more each day! I will revisit this later as we look at suffering.

When we walk in obedience to the Lord of Life, He creates some sacrifices out of our losses, as He did in my life, but many sacrifices must be willingly chosen as

He presents them to us. Just as Abraham chose, just as Hannah chose, just as Yeshua chose! God is a covenant-keeping God, and His ultimate sacrifice of His own son has given us the hope that never fails; nothing in this life will ever, in any shape or form, separate us from the love of our God that is in Christ Jesus our Lord.

Our Spiritual Key for the Journey Guidepost II: Sacrifice

Has your time for sacrifice come yet? Perhaps it will be choosing the road "less traveled" or living on the mission field in service, with little thought of material comfort. Listen to the Father's words to us all, below, and please absorb this truth: the fullness, the power, and the beauty of sacrifice increase as you press into your own. Please pray for the Father's meaning to be revealed to you, for your life, before reading the following listening prayer:

Listening Prayer

You are full because I AM your fullness. Your fullness is MY LOVE, and in the fullness of time, MY Love will be complete, perfect, teleios.

My thorns will be MY Glory, my kindness and strength producing the flashes of lightning around my shimmering countenance.

Oh, weak and humble children. Fear Not, I command you! My Presence is with you, I have filled you with living water in one day and I will transfuse this Blood of My Sacrifice, my suffering, my power of resurrection into you.

Peace, be still, rest, arms open wide. It will only hurt

for a moment, but the gift will last all eternity in my presence.

Take what you've been given and pour, pour, pour it out. It has no end. When joined by the angelic and the mundane, it multiplies infinitely. Remember the gift of Brokenness and Healing- only you will contain it. Only Our LOVE will one day proclaim and explain all.

My Arms are OUTSTRETCHED. My lightning fire now surrounds the earth. (An image is given of Him above the world and streams of light falling from Him. Divided flames are his streams of light not yet joined together –WAITING)

(Then, an image comes of many dots of light in clumps all over the earth, growing- but in the midst, a dark vortex as big as an ocean).

You are my grid of light growing between the longitudinal lines of fire, covering the earth, closing the gaps, and one day bridging the vortex of darkness completely and closing it off.

Your Abba Father.

Amen.

Psalm 29:7 (NIV): The voice of the Lord strikes with flashes of lightning.

(NASV) The voice of Jehovah cleaves the flames of fire.

Received December 4, 2016

Reflections

1. Ask yourself in every circumstance: what am I being asked to submit to because it is God's sovereign will and (it is inevitable) that it becomes part of my life?
2. Am I willing and able to release something of myself to Him as a holy sacrifice in this situation?
3. Am I sure that none of my ways of sacrifice are ego-centric and self-made, elevating me rather than glorifying the Father?
4. How has He called me to make sacrifices in my own life and walk this out on the road that I take, as part of virgin Israel going "Up to Jerusalem"?
5. Step into that choice willingly. Submit and do not resist the Sovereign God.

Guidepost III

Healing

Introduction

If the theme of this book is "Learning to walk in the way of Holiness for His Name's sake," then why is it important to discuss the topic of healing? Is this something that is integral to the process of sanctification and the pursuit of righteousness, following on the heels of living a sacrificial life, as discussed in the last chapter?

It is in the Character of God to Heal.

It seems to have always been on the mind of God to discipline and to heal, to wound and bind up. His hands are healing hands:

> 17 "Blessed is the one whom God corrects;
> so do not despise the discipline of the Almighty.
> 18 For He wounds, but He also binds up;
> He injures, but His hands also heal. Job 5:17-18

He corrects us, He disciplines us, He (allows) wounds, YET He heals our wounds, our infirmities, and the sicknesses of the body! Does this scripture shock you?

He is a God of compassion for His creation who would not have us faint away; rather, He says He would heal, guide, restore, and comfort those who mourn:

> I have seen their ways, but I will heal them;
> I will guide them and restore comfort to Israel's mourners
> ...Peace, peace to those far and near and I will heal them.
> Isaiah 57:18-19

He heals our ways, our sinful nature, and gives His Shalom.

Answer # 1 to the question introduced above: If it is the character of God to sacrifice Himself on the Cross and to heal His people, then it must be integral to our own character to do the same! To sacrifice, to be healed, and to become healers. It is essential to our own progress in sanctification if we want to become more and more closely aligned with Him.

Deeper Understanding of the Healing Words in Hebrew

There are many words that mean or are closely associated with *healing* in the Hebrew, and many more for *restore*. In the above scriptures, we see different shades of meaning when the English "heal" is used rather than the more accurate Hebrew translation. Job 5:17-18 is more accurately translated as "but his hands make whole." Strongs, 7495, tirpenah is a form of rapha (to heal) with this different meaning. In the second scripture quoted above, the meaning of "and I will heal them" is also *tirpenah*, so the idea of healing is expanded to bringing them to a place of wholeness.

Here are some of the many words used to indicate some form of healing in the Hebrew:

Yirpeel (pronounced yir-peh-EL) is a place in Bejamin, according to Strongs Hebrew Concordance 3416, which means God will heal. It is derived from the Hebrew root word *rapha*. It is found only one place in Joshua 18:27

Rapha (Strongs Concordance 7495) means to heal, to cure, in the context of physical healing, emotional restoration and spiritual renewal. Let's look at Isaiah 19:22 for a rich meaning in context:

"And the LORD will strike Egypt with a plague; He will strike them but heal them. They will turn to the LORD, and He will hear their prayers and heal them." The rich meaning here is that when Egypt learns to pray, healing will be theirs, and it is God's WILL.

Teshubah (Strongs Concordance 8666) means turning, often in the context of repentance, as in "I will heal your faithlessness" (NAS exhaustive concordance notes the root word is from Strongs 7725 shub; to turn back). Rarely, it also means to restore to a healthy condition (see Ex: 4:7 Orthodox Jewish Bible). When Moses put his hand back in his cloak and then took it out, it was turned again as his other basar (or "flesh") like the rest of his flesh. This was a sign the Lord used to heal Moses' faithlessness.

Arukah: healing, and restoration (Strongs Concordance 724). Isaiah 58:8: "Then your light will break out like the dawn, And your recovery will speedily spring forth" (NASB). The NIV says, "and your healing will quickly appear." In this context, i.e., the restoration of Israel, healing is on a much grander scale, which I think is conveyed in the NASB.

God is complex and multi-faceted, as the above words indicate. I am struck with the realization that almost every scripture refers to a type of restoration requiring a healing of faith and a closer walk with God. However, as a person in the "inner healing, freedom and restoration" ministry, I quickly learned that my Sovereign God is not a God to be questioned regarding His motives and actions when it comes to discipline and healing. We may study the scriptures intently regarding healing, and we will, and still... it seems that He has intentionally hidden from us the times and places of His healing revelation. He continues to work together with His faithful disciples to speak healing in Jesus' name and see the amazing manifestation of His power in the Name of Jesus. Our Lord God almighty, nonetheless, remains unsearchable.

Continuing the Journey In Israel

A few days into our journey, when we reached Jerusalem, the Lord had whispered to me, *"Healing is your guidepost. If you recognize and receive My power and presence to heal, you have seen the Father!"*

In Jerusalem

On our second day in Jerusalem, we had many times of devotion and saturation in His presence. We climbed the steps to the temple where Jesus walked, pausing to pray and plant seeds. We went to the western wailing wall and prayed. We walked the Herodian tunnel, passing by the ancient place of the Holy of Holies, now believed to be buried beneath the existing temple mount, and in silent awe, considered the ancient and sacred resting place of the Glory of God. After all that, we came to the Pool of Bethsaida:

2 Now there is in Jerusalem near the Sheep Gate a pool, which in Aramaic is called Bethesda and which is surrounded by five covered colonnades. 3 Here a great number of disabled people used to lie—the blind, the lame, the paralyzed. 5 One who was there had been an invalid for thirty-eight years. 6 When Jesus saw him lying there and learned that he had been in this condition for a long time, he asked him, "Do you want to get well?"

7 "Sir," the invalid replied, "I have no one to help me into the pool when the water is stirred. While I am trying to get in, someone else goes down ahead of me."

8 Then Jesus said to him, "Get up! Pick up your mat and walk."9 At once the man was cured; he picked up his mat and walked. John 5:2-8

14 Later Jesus found him at the temple and said to him, "See, you are well again. Stop sinning or something worse may happen to you." 15 The man went away and told the Jewish leaders that it was Jesus who had made him well. John 5:14-15

Is Sin the Root of Sickness?

It might sound like Jesus was telling this man that sin had been the root of his illness when He admonishes him to "stop sinning or something worse may happen to you." But we don't really know that, do we? We have extrapolated and assumed that's what Jesus meant. Often, we do this in an attempt to discern what the spiritual cause of one's illness may be as well as Jesus's power and motivation to heal. If we look at all the stories of healing by our Lord in Matthew 8 and 9, we learn that faith and God's forgiveness of our sin, as well as His desire and commandment to heal, all play a part at various times. However, Jesus made sure we heard clearly that *sin is not always* the cause of disease:

> "Master, whose sin caused this man's blindness," asked the disciples, "his own or his parents'?" "He was not born blind because of his own sin or that of his parents," returned Jesus, "but to show the power of God at work in him"..."I am the world's light, as long as I am in it."John 9:2-5

Healing Displays the Power, Glory, and Desire of God

Jesus simply desired to shine the light of God's glory by healing this man's blindness while He was in the world. We understand that in shining that light before the massive crowds of followers, many believed and found salvation in Christ. Jesus had the *authority*, the *power*, and the *position* as the Son of God to do exactly that. And then it was his desire to shine forth!

Jesus Demonstrates His Authority to Forgive Sin and to Heal, and He Recognizes Faith

In Matt 9:4-8, Jesus addresses the issue of His authority directly when He speaks to the doubting teachers of the law:

> [4] Knowing their thoughts, Jesus said, "Why do you entertain evil thoughts in your hearts? [5] Which is easier: to say, 'Your sins are forgiven,' or to say, 'Get up and walk'? [6] **But I want you to know that the Son of Man has authority on earth to forgive sins.**" So he said to the paralyzed man, "Get up, take your mat and go home." [7] Then the man got up and went home. [8] When the crowd saw this, they were filled with awe; and they praised God, who had given such authority to man.

I believe that the forgiveness of sins that Jesus speaks of is synonymous with healing in this situation by our Lord's words and actions. I have witnessed this in assisting seekers to work through their painful lives and emotional and physical conditions. However, is it always true; does God always heal in this way through the forgiveness of sins? No, He often responds primarily to the faith of the person requesting the healing (Mt. 8:9, Mt 9:18, Mt 9:22, Mt 9:29). Jesus addresses how much faith and perseverance is in the seeker, but He never makes it the only factor that affects the outcome of the believer's prayer for healing.

When Healing Did Not Occur

We all know that Paul prayed 3 times for his thorn in the flesh to be removed (2 Cor 12:8), and the Lord did not do so, to keep him from becoming conceited (1 Cor 12:7). Was that an actual thorn, an annoying cough, or a more serious physical condition? All we know for sure is that he was told, "My grace is sufficient for you." Paul also had to tell Timothy to drink a little wine for his frequent stomach aches (1 Tim 5:23). Finally, a friend named Trophimus was left behind in Miletus, Paul tells Timothy, because he was ill (2 Tim 4:20). There is no indication that any of these situations of ongoing illness resulted from Paul's or Timothy's lack of faith, timid prayers, or inability to persevere!

Because we are on this road up to Jerusalem and following the guideposts, I am seeking the connections between them. As referenced at the beginning of this third guidepost, we must all be living a sacrificial life of humility and be willing to accept what the Father has given us. I see Paul, Timothy, and Trophimus as examples of men who said, "Yes Lord, thy will be done, not my way but your way. I will serve you regardless of my health or lack of wellness. I place no demand on My Lord that He heal me so that I can do His will." This is sacrificial living.

Where Does Illness Originate?

Is God always the cause of injury and the healer of it, and is every wound and binding a discipline? (Job 15:18). Who allowed Satan to buffet Job? And who allowed the blind man to be born blind so that his healing would glorify God? Do we really know the answers to these questions? Although the answer seems to be God or Satan with God's permission, God's ways are not our ways, and "His thoughts are higher than ours." He is sovereign and omnipotent over all His creation.

> *"I make known the end from the beginning, from* ancient times, what is still to come. I say, 'My purpose will stand, and I will do all that I please' "* Isaiah 46:10

He knows the end from the beginning, and as Job says, *"I know that you can do all things; no plan of yours can be thwarted."* Job 42:2

It is very helpful to pause here and look at a summary of the will of God by R.C. Sproul:

1. The three meanings of the will of God:

*(a) **Sovereign decretive will** (Permission granted) the will by which God brings to pass whatsoever He decrees. This is hidden from us until it happens.*

*(b) **Preceptive will** (Perfect Will) is God's revealed law or commandments, (His precepts) which we have the power but not the right to break.*

*(c) **Will of disposition** (Perfect will) describes God's attitude or disposition. It reveals what is pleasing to Him.*

2. God's sovereign "permission" of human sin is not His moral approval.[5]

In summary, our God can decree healing for anyone

5   Chapter 22, pages 67-69, Essentials Truths Of The Christian Faith by R. C. Sproul © (Tyndale 1992)

at any time, in response to prayer or without anyone's prayer. He will also show us His will by revealing His laws and commandments. Leviticus 11-17 often reads like the Priests' medical manual from God, as He revealed some important public health regulations for the Israelites. Finally, God's perfect will, His attitude, or disposition is to heal us, to forgive us our sins, and to make us whole with Him and in Him. In Matthew 13:15b, Jesus was speaking about the fulfillment of Isaiah's prophecy (Isaiah 6:9-10):

> "...they might see with their eyes, hear with their ears, understand with their hearts and turn, <u>and I would heal them</u>."

I do not doubt that healing us is God's, the Son's, and the Holy Spirit's perfect will. God knew then and knows now how slowly man turns to Him. He allowed this hesitancy in us to develop from the beginning for His own purposes.

Under the new covenant, we are assured that we have been given the Spirit of Christ (John 16:13-15) and that we can search out and pray with the Holy Spirit, who is interceding for the saints and sometimes reveals His plans (leading us into all truth) and intentions to heal. Sometimes, He does not. And sometimes, He likes to show off and heal His children spontaneously! He promised, *"I will put my law in their minds and write it on their hearts. I will be their God, and they will be my people"* (Jer. 31:33). To which we add the assurance of 1 Cor. 2:16, as Paul writes about the way in which the spiritual man, taught by the Spirit, understands the things that come from the Spirit of God; **"*But we have the mind of Christ.*"**
And still:

> .... for true wisdom has two sides, can you fathom the mysteries of God? Can you probe the limits of the Almighty?" [Job 11:5-7]

Nothing in all creation is hidden from God's sight; Everything is uncovered and laid bare before the eyes of Him to whom we must give an account. Heb 4:13

I do remember from my Presbyterian catechism that God is omnipresent, omnipotent, and omniscient. I find that kind of all-knowing presence and power a comfort in times of difficult hardship, when healing has not come despite a multitude of prayers. It is then that I feel this truth:

Endure hardship as discipline. Heb 12:7

I have been disciplined (discipled, directed, guided) during hardship and love the Lord all the more for being present with me in it.

Some today do not believe this hardship or discipline includes illness:

One well-known person who has a tremendously fruitful ministry and has become a well-known teacher in the healing ministries has said:

"Scripture does not teach anywhere that God wants to use sickness to transform a person's character or produce repentance. "BUT" (emphasis added) God can produce good from the bad things he did not want in a person's life...God as any good father would, wants the best for His children, even when they are in circumstances in life that were not his will for them." (And yet he SEES it all before, during and after. Heb 4:13)

And yet:

- Jesus taught, "Stop sinning, or something worse may happen." One could easily assume that the blind man likely went home and repented of every sin he could remember committing from birth. I think that the firm directive from Jesus changed that blind man's character and produced repentance.

- Paul said that his thorn was not removed in order to keep him humble. His character was being chiseled and honed by the presence of this thorn.

The plain meaning of scripture is difficult for many to digest because it is so full of paradoxes and seeming contradictions. It all hinges on the "wants to." Does God <u>want</u> to use anything available to perfect His creation and bring us into a relationship that is totally dependent on Him and intimately connected?

Question: Does Scripture say God will heal?

Jeremiah 33:6 (NIV) *"'Nevertheless, I will bring health and healing to it; <u>I will heal my people</u> and will let them enjoy abundant peace and security.*

Matthew 10:1 (NIV) *Jesus called his twelve disciples to him and gave them authority to drive out impure spirits and <u>to heal every disease and sickness.</u>*

Malachi 4:2 (TLB) *"But for you who fear my name, the Sun of Righteousness will <u>rise with healing in his wings.</u> And you will go free, leaping with joy like calves let out to pasture.*

Isaiah 53:5 (NIV) *But he was pierced for our transgressions, he was crushed for our iniquities; the punishment that brought us peace was on him, and <u>by his wounds we are healed</u>.*

1 Peter 2:24 (NIV) *"He himself bore our sins" in his body on the cross, so that we might die to sins and live for righteousness; "by his wounds you have been healed."*

Psalm 103:2-3 (NIV) *Praise the Lord, my soul, and*

forget not all his benefits—who forgives all your sins and heals all your diseases.

Romans 8:11 (NIV) *And if the Spirit of him who raised Jesus from the dead is living in you, he who raised Christ from the dead will also give life to your mortal bodies because of his Spirit who lives in you.*

Answer to the question: ABSOLUTELY, Scripture says God heals us.

How?

- *Faith*
- *forgiveness*
- *God's desire and His Sovereign decreed will spoken and commanded on Earth as it is in Heaven; both play a role in healing.*

Let us now dig a little deeper and examine each of the above.

God's Sovereignty in Healing

Psalm 107:20 describes what happens when healing occurs; **"HE sent His WORD and healed them."**

It is critical to our comprehensive understanding of healing to get the fact that the heavy lifting of SENDING the WORD and the actual HEALING are God's part. He does it according to His sovereign will, decreed or perfect (His disposition), which He sometimes does in partnership with those of His children who have prayed in faith, believing that they will receive.

Never doubt that **He is sovereign**:

"I make known the end from the beginning, from ancient times, what is still to come. I say, 'My purpose will stand, and I will do all that I please.'" Isaiah 46:10

He knows the end from the beginning, and as Job says, "I know that you can do all things; no plan of yours can be thwarted."
Job 42:2

He also heals to partner with us in our faith.

What's faith got to do with it if it's all about His Sovereign will?

- Romans 10:17 Consequently, faith comes from hearing the message, and the message is heard through the word about Christ.

- In Luke 18:8, Jesus asks, "When the son of man comes, will he really find faith on the earth?" He asks the question because He wants us to know how important this is to Him: Have we HEARD?

- It's not about "how much" but in WHOM we have faith. Do not navel-gaze to measure faith; find out who Jesus is and believe. This is the work we must do.

- "To them, God has chosen to make known among the Gentiles the glorious riches of this mystery, which is Christ in you, the hope of glory..." (Col 1:27); "I am the vine, you are the branches... apart from me you can do nothing" (John 15:5). Understand these truths, and you will walk in faith.

- "God has dealt to each one a measure of faith" (Rom 12:3). You have been given that measure which enables you to do what you have been called to do! According to Matthew 17:20, "If you have faith as a mustard seed, you will say to this mountain, move from here to there, and it will move;

nothing will be impossible for you."

- Faith is an active, not passive, <u>resting</u> in the Lord. You don't have to conjure up your faith, for you have the faith of Jesus Christ already within you. (every good gift has been given!) Then, the works of faith become a natural outpouring (James 2:26).

Let's look at that famous scripture in which Jesus states that the blind man's faith has made him whole. In Luke 18:39-42, we read of the seemingly spontaneous and unsolicited healing of the blind man. But even here in this exchange, we witness three things: 1) the blind man pleads for mercy from Jesus; 2) he is immediately obedient and responsive to the Lord; 3) he acknowledges Jesus as the one who can give him sight and then Jesus heals him, afterward commending him for his faith. I would have to conclude that this man's faith was active as he interacted with the Lord.

Forgiveness

I believe that to forgive puts us in perfect alignment with the most essential characteristic of God. Faith is so huge and yet faith does not perform a miracle in a vacuum. Jesus brings healing into our lives through His loving desire in concert with forgiveness.

Forgiveness is so critical to our healing and to the placement and positioning of our body, mind, soul, and spirit into a healing relationship with our Lord that a separate chapter was required. Please see guidepost number ten.

It's ok to jump ahead if you need to, but please come back here because there is a lot more!

Present Day: My Healing Testimony at Bethsaida, Jerusalem

While at the pool of Bethsaida (Bethesda), I sat among many herbal bushes: sage, lavender, rosemary, bay, and more. I knelt to bury a mustard seed among those bushes, placing a leaf from each on top of the seed, and this verse popped into my *mind: "And a tree will be there and its leaves will be for the healing of the nations"* (Rev 22:2). I let this be my prayer as I thought about the many nations that are raised up in anger and intolerance for Israel and simply added, "Heal me as well, Lord." This was a very brief prayer with faith, literally the size of a mustard seed, and yet when I stood up to go, my entire body was flooded with energy and renewed in an amazing way! I couldn't believe it as I recalled how I had been exhausted and footsore, ready to retreat to the hotel for a long afternoon nap and just write off the day to old age. Even my feet now felt like I could walk a hundred miles. The change was visible to everyone around me, and this amazing healing lasted throughout the day, into the next, and for the rest of our time in Jerusalem. Then I recalled that at the western wall, I had prayed Mary's prayer, echoing the praises and gratitude that I am blessed among women to be a chosen vessel for my Lord's Holy Spirit. To be in His presence and intimate with God is to receive His gifts, His love, and His healing.

Healed From Suicidal Depression

Other times in my life when healing has come in an almost instantaneous, spontaneous way came to mind. One instance was especially significant to me. Please keep in mind that I am writing this self-reflection from the viewpoint of an educated and licensed therapist, as well as one totally in love and devoted to following Jesus for the last 53 years!

This healing came as if decreed sovereignly by God, because there was no prayer immediately preceding. It occurred as I listened to a testimony of miraculous healing from bipolar disorder, and God said very clearly, although not audibly, "This is for you; you will never have to go around that mountain again." I immediately knew that He meant that the possibility of another deep, dark suicidal depression had left me forever. After a lifetime of facing these oppressive spirits of death and cycling through normal times, hypomanic times, and suicidal times, it was such a tremendous relief that I scarcely dared even to believe it. But I did believe Him with absolute confidence and began to share immediately what I had heard deep within me: that I was indeed mentally, emotionally, and physically healed of depression. Gradually, over the next five months, with my doctor's watchful eye over me, I even reduced and eliminated my medicine. Eleven years later, I continue to have such peace and to enjoy His presence that I know that I have the Spirit of Peace dwelling within me! He has granted me His Shalom. "I have not been given a spirit of fear, but (I have been given His Spirit) of love, power and a sound mind" (2 Timothy 1:7). So that "I can take every thought captive and make it obedient to Christ" (2 Cor 10:5).

For about a year before this healing occurred, I had been set free from multiple oppressing spirits and crippling mindsets such as fear, control, rejection and worthlessness, word curses, addiction, and generational ties to addiction, alcohol abuse, rebellion, and suicide. My experience taught me that these "onion" layers peeled back over time can open our hearts to God's spontaneous movement to heal. In addition, I had the benefit of about five years of medical care prior to all of this, with an excellent psychiatrist who was an expert in the spectrum of bipolar disorders. So, with medication, I had reached a level of comfort and emotional stability that was very different from the past. That stability came with the price of some emotional numbness, however, which is a common complaint of those who are medicated with mood stabilizers. I continue to give credit to all the directions from which I received aid toward my healing.

However, without God's inner healing and spiritual freedom, I could not, 11 years later, continue to be completely free and happy without any type of psychogenic medication. That just does not happen!

This change and healing in me have become the backbone of my current ministry of inner healing and freedom from oppression. There have been numerous other healings, both physical and emotional, entirely through the grace and forgiveness of my Savior, but I could not be in ministry today had He not chosen to heal me emotionally and physically that day and cancel that enormous curse over my life.

As is often the way in healing, the Lord reveals and heals, then He reveals even more! Part of my continued progress and solidity in my "aftercare" spiritual growth was a sudden insight that Father gave me one day. I learned that a spirit of self-pity had, at some point, taken up its position over me, holding on to the foothold that I had provided. This makes perfect sense psychologically when we look at the effects of trauma in anyone's life at any age. The subconscious trauma memory is a trigger that continues within our soul to activate the pain, fear, terror, and dread of that past, such as my sister's suicide, my father's death, my own suicide attempts, abortion, divorce, my son's death, abandonment, and more. The spirit of self-pity was more than happy to accommodate my wounds with a constant soothing and seductive reminder that I was going to "drown in these losses, I should always expect more loss, and I should feel very, very sorry for myself because no one else could ever understand the depths of my pain." Self-pity is ugly and all-consuming. It is pride in disguise because it is "all about me"! For me, just knowing and recognizing its presence allowed me to renounce it and pray it away, breaking every agreement that I had ever made with it, cutting its bindings and pulling out every deep root in the mighty name of Yeshua. It left, I closed the door to my spirit and sealed it shut, and the last shreds of depression departed. Now I can pray for others in the same way, and it is such a blessing to see healing spread out like pools of shimmering light beneath the footsteps of our Lord.

The key for the Journey Guidepost III Healing:

Whether or not you have experienced healing in your life yet is really not germane; if you are looking, you will eventually see and believe Yeshua still heals today. **Go to the Waters of Bethesda as you imagine them in your Spirit mind. Step into them now, and Yeshua will stir the waters himself.**

Just the other day, as I sat outside, overlooking the river, His love whispered:

Songs and winds, rapids roar, light-like
In glistening radiant hues of verdant green-
ignite together to Speak my mind.
My thought of life and power within you,
my thought of you, to you and for you is healing-
Healing power is released in the froth of white water
that chases the current downstream,
Is released in the bird song that answers and argues
from its high place of strength!

*Speak life and clamorous harmonies of brilliant
eggshell blue
Punctuate the canopy of translucent pale lime
springtime...
This is my voice, and it has always whispered life
over you
And through you when you least ask or expect it.
Give it away! Always give it away.
Go to the pool of Bethsaida everyday
Step into the waters and I will stir them!!
Do Not Wait.*

"I AM the Lord who heals you" (Ex 15:26).

As a clinical counselor, I believe strongly in the use of psychiatric drugs and never recommend reducing or eliminating them without a doctor's supervision. In any healing, listen to God and then return to your doctor for direction and supervision. Shalom.

Reflections

Do you see the progress of the guideposts that lead from a new covenant relationship with your Lord Jesus to living a sacrificial life, to receiving healing and freedom from bondage?

1. We have seen that faith, forgiveness, His desire, and/or His commandment preceded healing in the stories in Matt 8 and 9. What have you personally experienced as a precedent to healing?
2. Why did Jesus do the work of healing in John 9:2-5 and what was the result? Do you feel that this is why the church today seeks the gifts of healing or the obvious manifestation of healings today?
3. Is God or Satan always the cause of injury or sickness? Who allowed Satan to buffet Job? Who al-

lowed the man's blindness to exist in order to show God's Glory? Is there evidence that shows this as God's perfect will or His permissive will?

4. Have you been discipled by God and brought closer into relationship with Him because of your wounds, injuries, or illnesses? If so, what have you discovered about yourself, God, and the world we live in?

5. Does healing depend on you, your initiative, your faith, your persistence? Or is it in God's hands? (caution, this is a trick question)

Healing Scripture Statements

Jeremiah 33:6 (NIV) "'Nevertheless, I will bring health and healing to it; I will heal my people and will let them enjoy abundant peace and security.'"

Matthew 10:1 (NIV) Jesus called His twelve disciples to him and gave them authority to drive out impure spirits and to heal every disease and sickness.

Malachi 4:2 (TLB) "But for you who fear my name, the Sun of Righteousness will rise with healing in His wings. And you will go free, leaping with joy like calves let out to pasture."

Isaiah 53:5 (NIV) But he was pierced for our transgressions, he was crushed for our iniquities; the punishment that brought us peace was on him, and by his wounds we are healed. **1 Peter 2:24 (NIV)**[24] "He himself bore our sins" in his body on the cross, so that we might die to sins and live for righteousness; "by his wounds you have been healed."

Psalm 103:2-3 (NIV) Praise the Lord, my soul, and forget not all his benefits—who forgives all your sins and heals all your diseases.

Romans 8:11 (NIV) And if the Spirit of him who raised Jesus from the dead is living in you, he who raised Christ from the dead will also give life to your mortal bodies because of[1] his Spirit who lives in you

Psalm 107:20 (NKJV) He sent His word and healed them, And delivered *them* from their destructions.

Psalm 118:16-17 (NKJV) The right hand of the Lord is exalted; The right hand of the Lord does valiantly. I shall not die, but live, And declare the works of the Lord.

Matthew 8:17b (NKJV) "He Himself took our infirmities, and bore our sicknesses."

John 6:63 It is the Spirit who gives life; the flesh profits nothing. The words that I speak to you are spirit, and *they* are life.

Romans 4:17b (TLB) And this promise is from God himself, who makes the dead live again and speaks of future events with as much certainty as though they were already past.

Mark 11:24 (NIV) Therefore I tell you, whatever you ask for in prayer, believe that you have received it, and it will be yours.

Proverbs 4:20-22 (TLB) Listen, son of mine, to what I say. Listen carefully. Keep these thoughts ever in mind; let them penetrate deep within your heart, for they will mean real life for you and radiant health

Deut.7:15 (TLB) And the Lord will take away all your sickness and will not let you suffer any of the diseases of Egypt you remember so well; he will give them all to your enemies.

Luke 18: 40-42 (NIV) Jesus asked him, "What do you want me to do for you?" He said, "Lord, I want to see," he replied. Then Jesus said to him, "Receive your sight; your faith has healed you" (other translations state, "Your faith has made you well").

Guidepost IV

The Lord Our Righteousness

While in Jerusalem at the Olive Tree Hotel, some friends and I were praying and listening to the still small voice of the Lord:

My guidepost of Righteousness will test the waters of moral ambiguity and evaporate the sloth of forgetfulness. Soon, a thick residue of waste that pollutes will choke the life from places where righteousness has died. The high places when one comes Up to Jerusalem will remain for those whose judgment has not yet come. Seek, and you shall find.

Followed by Jeremiah 33:15-16:

[15] In those days and at that time I will cause a **righteous Branch** to spring up for David; and he shall execute justice and righteousness in the land. [16] In those days Judah will be saved and Jerusalem will live in safety. And this is the name by which it will be called: "**The Lord Our Righteousness.**"

In order to understand the powerful warning of the above listening word, I will try to unpack the meaning of righteousness and then look at moral ambiguity.

The message given is tied into the Jeremiah 33:15-16 scripture, so I looked at this first. In his commentary on the scripture, Matthew Poole states, "The Branch of Righteousness here spoken of can only mean Christ who is called a Branch out of the stem of Jesse in Isa 11:1 and a righteous Branch in Jer. 23:5." "In those days" is commonly understood to refer to the end times. This much of the above scripture is clear: Jesus Christ has come and will come again to reign and rule from Jerusalem. But why does Jeremiah say in the last sentence, "and this is the name by which it (*Judah and Jerusalem*) shall be called, "The Lord Our Righteousness"?

Another commentator, Matthew Henry, states that "the promises of the covenant shall have full accomplishment in the gospel Israel... all that walk according to the gospel rule are made to be the Israel of God, on whom shall be peace and mercy. (But) let us not despise the families which were of old, the chosen people of God." What I hear in this quote is that the gospel of Israel was first for and in the land; Judah and Jerusalem will forever be renowned for that which was born there in Bethlehem and came into the fullness of His Righteousness on the cross in Jerusalem. Christians will be welcomed in from the four corners of the earth, and all of Israel will be saved as well (Romans 11:26).

I feel certain that there is no holier place on earth than Jerusalem. His presence is always at the Pool of Bethsaida; I am a personal witness of that, and He is strongly felt in other holy places like the Garden of Gethsemane. Thousands of seekers have met Jesus in astonishing ways throughout His land and what will soon be His eternal home in the City of our God. And, of course, Jerusalem means the City of Peace or the "Abode of Peace."

We know this: when we live in Christ, we are abiding in Him, who is our "Abode" of peace! We are called by our

Lord to "abide in me," and He will place His word within us to answer that which we pray for in Jesus' Name. Of course, as we abide IN HIM, we will ask what the Father's desire is, as well. In the deepest sense of the word, entering into GOD's rest, or Shalom, is entering into His will, His completion or wholeness, and the righteousness who is our Lord Jesus Christ.

In the mystery of God, we also enter into the land called "The Lord our Righteousness," where it was fully accomplished.

Righteousness Defined

First, let us define the meaning of righteousness. Primarily, it means "right standing before God." But this definition opens us up to so much more when we try to comprehend what right standing before our Creator—He whose breath gave us life, who made the universe—actually means. It must include grace or suspended judgment; in other words, the judgment for my sins, my choices to turn away from Him, has been satisfied, and I am spurred on the path of progressive sanctification. Once we gain this knowledge, it is sometimes followed by an immediate awareness of intimacy with God, but more often, a journey of years and a thousand prayers begins. However, the truth that I can enter into the presence of God, that sin has been removed, and that I can enter the Holy of Holies, eventually brings me awestruck to my knees! This is such an incredible truth that a mere definition cannot begin to describe and encompass the spiritual life we have been given in the Lord our Righteousness!

So, I have to pause here and ask, "What is Our Condition without Christ?"

"Lord God, I long to write all you have for us regarding the guidepost of righteousness," I pray, but first, place me under your cosmic scaled microscope to "see if there be any sinful way in me" and lead me in the way everlasting. As you do so, I am stripped bare again and made aware of my wretched condition in my human state. I recall a vivid inner vision you once gave, in which I saw myself chained to the wall of a disgusting, filthy, narrow alley filled with garbage, dressed in rags and covered with years of grime, hopelessly hanging by manacles around my wrists, neck, and feet. Far worse than any movie image of Scrooge awaiting the ghost of the future that haunts him or the desperate children hidden beneath its robes. In my dream/vision, I could look out at the street and the passers-by but do and say nothing to release myself from those chains! I am reminded of the scripture that says: *All of us have become like one who is unclean, and all our righteous acts are like filthy rags; we all shrivel up like a leaf, and like the wind our sins sweep us away* (Isaiah 64:6). This vivid picture of the horrid and hopeless condition in which I exist, as does all of mankind, has never left me. So how can one such as I write about the Lord our Righteousness?

This awareness of my wretched condition without Christ leads me to pray:

Father, you have taught us in the scriptures and through the history of the nation of Israel, your people, what is right and what is wrong. Carefully and with great specificity, you took pains to write your commandments and give them to Moses. Yet, like the Israelites of old, we continually, as individuals, as your body of Christ, as a society, or as an entire nation, attempt to rewrite your commandments in our own "image" in order to please ourselves. How your heart must break, Lord, for those whose feet are mired in moral ambiguity; the wasteland, the thick residue, the sloth that pollutes, then chokes out your life within us! And yet:

"God chose the lowly things of this world and the despised things--and the things that are not--to nullify the things that are." 1 Cor 1:28-30

My gentle savior was telling me that even I, as lowly as I knew I was, truly was chosen by Him...

Key Scriptures on Righteousness

Naturally, the scriptures give us the best definition of righteousness! Beginning, for me, with this simple statement: *God made him who had no sin to be sin for us, so that in him we might become the righteousness of God.* 2 Cor 5:21 *And,*

"He condemned sin in the flesh, 4 that the righteous requirement of the law might be fulfilled in us who do not walk according to the flesh but according to the Spirit. 5 For those who live according to the flesh set their minds on the things of the flesh, but those who live according to the Spirit, the things of the Spirit" (Rom 8:3-5) ... furthermore 10 And if Christ is in you, the body is dead because of sin, but your spirit is alive (or gives life) because of righteousness. Rom 8:10

Another version of this scripture reads: *If Christ lives in you, you will live. Though your body will die because of sin, the Spirit gives you life. The Spirit does this because you have been made right with God* (Rom 8:10, NIRV). This is our not-yet-glorified but no less amazing position now.

21 But now, apart from the law, the righteousness of God has been made known, to which the Law and the Prophets testify. 22 This righteousness is given through faith in h Jesus Christ to all who believe. There is no difference between Jew

and Gentile, 23for all have sinned and fall short of the glory of God, 24and all are justified freely by his grace through the redemption that came by Christ Jesus. Rom 3:21-24

This is very important to understand that we have been given the gift of righteousness. It is imputed to us by the Lord, which, in theological circles, is referred to as *positional* righteousness. We are not under the same weighty requirement of the law—obsessive obedience—as the ancient Jews felt they were. They believed they had to strive to obey each and every minute law given both in scripture and devised by years of pharisaical rulers. No! We have this gift of grace because of Jesus Christ through our faith in Him. We have the Father and Him alone to praise and thank that He has allowed us to receive the Gift of the Holy Spirit through the coming, the death, and the resurrection of our Lord.

> "… in reference to your former manner of life, you lay aside the old self, which is being corrupted in accordance with the lusts of deceit, 23 and that you be renewed in the spirit of your mind, 24 and put on the new self, which in the likeness of God has been created in righteousness and holiness of the truth." Ephesians 4:22-24

We cannot attain the righteousness that is required of us, but we do <u>not</u> worry excessively about the Lord's warning: *"For I tell you that unless your righteousness surpasses that of the Pharisees and the teachers of the law, you will certainly not enter the kingdom of heaven"* (Matt 5:20). The Pharisees did have the righteousness of the law. As RC Sproul describes them, they were evangelical, passionate believers, students of the word, disciplined in prayer and tithing, and obedient to the letter of the law, <u>*yet without the spirit*</u>. This is the type of righteousness that Jesus expects us to exceed, knowing that He himself will be the giver of the gift of the spirit.

Rather, we desire with our whole spirit, mind, and soul to follow His commandments, and we depend on the presence, power, and guidance of the Holy Spirit to change, convict, direct, and closely align us to Jesus' own righteousness.

Definition of Moral Ambiguity

Since the Word given at the beginning of this guidepost is that His righteousness would "test the waters of moral ambiguity," it is helpful to now define this terminology. It has helped me to understand what the Lord was charging us with and to further develop and explain this issue.

Definition: Moral ambiguity presents an <u>ethical dilemma</u> where any given complex has a whole array of <u>moral dimensions</u>.

> **Moral Ambiguity**- Urban Dictionary: lack of clarity in ethical decision-making. That is, when an issue, situation, or question has <u>moral dimensions</u> or implications, but the decidedly "moral" action to take is unclear, either due to conflicting principles, ethical systems, <u>or situational perspectives</u>.

> **Ethical dilemma** or ethical paradox is a decision-making problem between two possible moral imperatives, neither of which is unambiguously acceptable or preferable. The complexity arises out of the <u>situational conflict</u> in which obeying one would result in transgressing another.

Most of us would likely equate moral ambiguity with a post-Christian cultural perspective that says there is no absolute truth and denies the truth of the scripture emphatically. This is part of the problem. However, it doesn't adequately address the fact that within the community of Christian Bible believers, there exist many ethical dilemmas and a whole array of moral dimensions.

Moral ambiguity is the polar opposite of the life of righteousness in the City of Jerusalem and the land of Judah, as promised by the prophet Isaiah in 32:15-20, in the days to come when Jesus is restored to His throne. That fortress and land will be abandoned, says Isaiah:

> [15] till the Spirit is poured on us from on high,
> and the desert becomes a fertile field,
> and the fertile field seems like a forest.
> [16] The LORD's justice will dwell in the desert,
> And his righteousness [will] live in the fertile field.
> [17] The **fruit of that righteousness** will **be peace**;
> its **effect** will **be quietness** and **confidence** forever.
> [18] My people will live in peaceful dwelling places,
> in **secure homes**, in **undisturbed places of rest.**

This is the promise of God and the life He promises to His righteous ones who will live in a righteous place in direct contrast to moral ambiguity.

My Testimony

What is the essence of that moral ambiguity we personally struggle with? There were many areas of my life that were awash with vague and lazy morals, actions, thoughts, and beliefs for much of my life. Even as I defined myself as a Christ follower who was active in ministry, to my shame (because the enemy was overly invested in this lie, I felt shame), I resorted to fancy "footwork" in my apologetics for the faith to the young people I knew who, as young adults, were rapidly leaving their Christian faith in the dust. I confess I did not have the courage to tell them that Jesus Christ, the knowledge of Him, and the acceptance of His sacrificial life, death, and resurrection are absolutely the only salvation for all peoples and for all times. I wished to believe that there was some way that the unreached masses and those who have denied Christ could know "The Way, the Truth, and the Life," perhaps by some mystical spiritual revelation between life and death. Of course, there is no scripture that gives us such assurance, and my ambiguity did nothing to encourage anyone in the faith. Instead, I left a mess that I have been trying to clean up for many decades.

A factor that relates to my ambiguity, spiritual oppression, is not understood by the secular world, nor in much of the Christian world either. The fact is that I have grown so much stronger since receiving complete freedom in Christ through deliverance from the oppressors in my life, such as people pleasing, rejection, and fear of abandonment, that my strength as a true witness has multiplied. Sadly, I now find the door in some minds nearly closed to the full truth. God's promises are true and unambiguous in regard to my children, however, and I have no fear about their ultimate salvation. He has a plan!

Occult Interference: In addition, in retrospect, I see that although I had changed my conscious beliefs about who my Lord really was when I accepted Christ, there was a spirit of the occult that still clouded my thinking. This was with me since my early days of seeking, before Christ, when I experimented with the "Great I AM" theosophical beliefs and was an initiate of the Maharishi Mahesh Yogi, who popularized Transcendental Meditation and led the Beatles, among thousands of others, down that path. I will address deliverance from oppression later in more detail, but there are such footholds as these which, once opened as young people, do need to be definitively closed and barricaded by the presence of the Word and the Holy Spirit within us.

Because others in my generation have also experienced their children leaving the faith, I want to acknowledge that no matter how strong a parent's personal testimony and witness may be, our children are choosing other paths. They are bombarded with the philosophies of this world, chiefly of humanism in this age, that impact their thinking throughout every system of secular education, the media, and cultural institutions. No one factor bears the responsibility for their educated decisions, their rebellious decisions, or their apathy.

Fortunately, for all of us, we have a God who forgives and who keeps promises and has a plan that will not harm us or our children but *"works for the good of those who love him and are called according to his purpose"* (Rom 2:28). He challenges me daily to speak the Truth, never prevaricate, evade, beat around the bush, hedge, dodge the issue, equivocate, waffle, hem and haw or shillyshally! I will not knowingly speak false or misleading words now, and I trust that *"For those God foreknew he also predestined to be conformed to the likeness of his Son, that he might be the first born among many brothers"* (Rom 8:29). This includes my children and all the hungry seekers I meet.

Ambiguity in the Body

We have been discussing the righteousness within the individual member of the body of Christ. But what happens when the body, the church, or any group attempts to enact or enforce what they believe is righteousness? In our present-day world, just as in the past through the Pharisees, Satan attempts to pervert the idea of righteousness in those who seek after unattainable purity through their own power. Just as ISIS, then HAMAS, all the Iranian proxies, and others in recent history, like the Nazis, have used horrific, murderous means against those considered impure: Christians, Jews, homosexuals, women caught in adultery or out of their traditional role; all may fall under the sword of terror or persecution. Christians, whether justly or not, have persecuted other Christians; even our own Puritans, for example, identified some women who manifested certain behaviors in the spirit as witches, and they were put to death.

Example from Bible History: What Happened Here?

In the past, the Israelites went to desperate extremes to enact the Righteousness of God; Judges 19-21 tells the story of the Levite and his concubine. After she was raped and murdered in a town of Israelites, the Levite asks the nation to avenge this murder. Unambiguously, they do so by wiping out the entire tribe of Benjamin, except for 600 men, because the leaders had refused to turn over the guilty parties. Over time and at least three battles, at least 100,000 men die. God had been sought and seemingly had directed them to enact this revenge. It echoes the language of the historical battles as well as the punishment for sin where God commands His people, "You must purge the evil from among you."

Now, there comes the ethical dilemma of how the law of Deuteronomy 5 was enforced. The rape and murder revenge act is followed by the mass murder of yet another tribe at Jabesh Gilead because the inhabitants had not joined Israel in their war against the Benjamites. The Israelites are feeling poorly about possibly annihilating part of God's chosen people, so the nation reserves 400 virgins from the second tribe to give to the Benjamites so they can re-populate. Does this make any sense to anyone? There is more, but you get the idea. I encourage you to read the entire account yourself! The moral ambiguity has become a thick soup, a wasteland, and a bloody morass, as murder leads to more murder. Although attempting to purify the nation of potential rapists and murderers resulted in some fasting and prayers before God, seeking His will, the appalling consequences of war and genocidal actions are epic. The Jews failed, I believe, miserably at this attempt to enforce righteousness on the nations. As this story was written and re-written over the ages, I earnestly believe that God intended His people to learn the lesson that a Messiah was desperately needed and would someday give them the New Covenant. Indeed, they would be crying out for their Messiah, "LORD SAVE US!" In that day, when the Law would be written on every man's heart by the power and the presence of the Holy Spirit and enabled through Christ's righteousness imbued in us, a radical change would come over mankind that would be the beginning of His righteousness covering the whole earth. Isaiah prophesized in chapter 32:15-17 that after the destruction of Jerusalem, it would become a wasteland "till the Spirit is poured upon us from on high, and the desert becomes fertile, and Justice will dwell in the desert... the fruit of righteousness will be peace, the effect of righteousness will be quietness and confidence forever." The Lord is our Righteousness in the power of the Holy Spirit!

Groupthink: Another Explanation. We now live in a society riddled with violence, and there seems to be no end in sight. Traditionally, in this nation, the rule of law and a strong police force kept order, but they now seem to be diluted, laws rewritten to minimize consequences or disregarded completely.

There is a psychological phenomenon called group-think **that** occurs within a group of people **in which the desire for harmony or conformity results in an irrational or dysfunctional** decision-making **outcome. Group members try to minimize conflict and reach a consensus decision by suppressing dissenting viewpoints, and by isolating themselves from outside**

influences. Irving Janis of Yale University who pioneered this research stated, "I use the term groupthink…to refer to the mode of thinking that persons engage in when *concurrence-seeking* **becomes so dominant in a cohesive ingroup that it tends to override realistic appraisal of alternative courses of action. Groupthink is a term (similar) to the newspeak vocabulary George Orwell used in his dismaying world of** *1984.* In that context, groupthink refers to a deterioration in mental efficiency, reality testing and moral judgments as a result of group pressures." He went on to write: *"groupthink is likely to result in irrational and dehumanizing actions directed against outgroups."*[6] Isn't this very much like the culture in the Western "civilized" nations of today?

Obviously, the evil one, who is still roaming about and attempting to devour us, is the source of the problem. In our "post-Christian" sophisticated world, Satan has been discarded too often as a quaint but outdated explanation of evil. God clearly knows all and used the evil Satan inspires in people as part of His master plan. He always has a plan, and we can pull back far enough from the details and gain His perspective (2 Cor 5:16). But has groupthink affected today's generation, me, or even modern Israel?

Testimony Time

What "groupthink" or our culture has not produced is a movement to draw anyone closer to intimacy with God through righteousness. My own experience in the moral morass and cult-like atmosphere of the Eastern religions of the 1960s was the making of a disillusioned, depressed, and lonely young hippie, still amoral, resorting again to

---

6   Wikipedia, "Groupthink" article and overview, en.n.wikipedia.org. (Credited to Wiki Education Foundation)

alcohol and drugs, who cried out on the beach one night, "Lord, if you are real, show me!" It took time, but He did put my life in motion, taking me to the place where some real genuine "Jesus Freaks" and mature members of the Charismatic movement would introduce me to the truth, the Lord, Jesus, my Yeshua, My Messiah, My Savior. The Lord, my righteousness! For me, one of the first noticeable changes in my soul and spirit was an amazing peace because I knew He had the answers; He was my truth because He was THE truth. All the searching I'd felt was my responsibility no longer burdened me with the insufferable weight of ambiguity.

Israel 2017

While in Jerusalem, we saw how the subset of ultra-conservative orthodox Jews isolated themselves in their quarter of the old city of David. Some cultural pressure may be at work here. They dress differently, follow carefully designated laws and rituals, and purge all impure modern cultural influences from their community. So strongly do they feel about protecting their "righteousness before God" that they will even jeer at, spit at, or throw stones at people who wander into their streets inappropriately dressed. (I think it is chiefly the young men who do this). What is this?

Is there any righteousness in sects, cults, or religious groups who keep themselves pure in such a way, attempting to avoid all moral ambiguity? Is the presence of the Lord, our Righteousness, in Jerusalem? Unequivocally, YES, and He invites each of us to enter into that righteousness as we enter into Him, there in Jerusalem as much as anywhere on the earth, if not more so. Does He encourage spitting and jeering at those who do not conform? NO, but because they continue to seek righteousness through compliance or conformity with the letter of rabbinical law, they have not been set free to recognize the hopeless limitations of the flesh.

However, regarding the ultra-orthodox:

> Brothers and sisters, with all my heart I long for the people of Israel to be saved. I pray to God for them. [2] I can tell you for certain that they really want to serve God. But how they are trying to do it is not based on knowledge. [3] They didn't know that <u>God's power</u> makes people right with himself. <u>They tried to get right with God in their own way. They didn't do it in God's way.</u> [4] Christ has fulfilled everything the law was meant to do. So now everyone who believes can be right with God. (in right standing) ^{Rom 10:1-4}

In other words, righteous.
A Prayer:

> *Lord, it is difficult and painful to see this struggle in the holy city and know your heart breaks for your people who love you, who have the "law and the prophets," as Paul wrote, who yearn to see their Messiah come, yet have a veil drawn over their eyes. I pray that out of those streets of Jerusalem will rise a new generation of Jews: rabbis, men and women, a people fulfilled, who will see beyond the veil and into the true bleeding, sacrificial, and righteous heart of God their Father and their Lord Yeshua. In the mighty Name of Yeshua the Messiah, Amen!*

Our Goal: The Clear and Unambiguous Righteousness of God

We have to continue somehow until the Lord returns, so what do we do? The righteous community, body of Christ, society, or nation we all desire will come when

His kingdom comes and His government is established over all the nations of the world. Until then, we carefully examine what is being done, but we "judge no one from a worldly point of view" (2 Cor 5:16). We hesitate to judge those within the body without the clear lens of Love.

> ➤ This is why we cannot grow into such depth of understanding without the Holy Spirit; we do not love others as God does, we do not have righteousness in our DNA, and our natural judgments are worthless. We have been given the first guidepost, the New Covenant in Christ so that God has access to our hearts and He is writing His law within us.
>
> ➤ Only His love can lead the sinner into redemption and replace the mind of the natural man with the mind of Christ. His love was poured out in sacrifice upon the cross. We live to love sacrificially, as in the second guidepost.
>
> ➤ Thirdly, the Christian who is receiving the miracle of healing and change within his own life can position himself to see the moral ambiguity, the pain, and the chaos in the community around him.
>
> ➤ Only the individual, compelled by the indwelling ministry of the Spirit of God, can seek and be filled with the righteousness of God that will pull him and his community who have chosen salvation out of the sloth of moral ambiguity.
>
> ➤ In addition:

[15] But the spiritual man [the spiritually mature Christian] judges all things [questions, examines, and applies what the Holy Spirit reveals], yet is himself judged by no one [the unbeliever cannot judge and understand the believer's spiritual nature]. [16] For who has known the mind and purposes of the Lord, so as to instruct Him? But we have the mind of Christ [to be guided by His thoughts and purposes] 1 Corinthians 2:15-16, AMP

This is truly what we do; we have the mind of Christ. If you just do not feel you are there yet, seek and ask and keep on knocking. If anyone lacks wisdom he should ask for it and it will be given (James 1:5). Begin now to learn to listen to the Lord and know that He is speaking to you always. He longs for that intimate relationship with you! Begin now.

Hope in Recent Years

Today, I spoke to a friend of mine who now lives in Israel. He spoke about the Lord's movement in very recent months, causing 67 Jewish rabbis to meet Yeshua at the Wailing Wall while in prayer and accepting Him as their Lord and Savior! The same prayer He put in my heart the very day our plane set down in Tel Aviv He has been answering, not just in this moment, but in His time and for His purposes since before His nation was reborn in its historic homeland. The first well-known, public Messianic Jewish Rabbi, Joseph Rabinowitz, had a life-changing encounter with Yeshua and accepted Him as his Messiah on the Mount of Olives in 1882. Three years later, the first assemblies of the Israelites of the New Covenant were held in Moldova (Your People Shall Be My People, pg. 134, D. Finto), and God is continuing to move in mighty ways today to bring His plan to fruition.

Encouragement in Listening Prayer

This is how the Lord would encourage His righteous children. All of us who believe and received His gift of eternal life are called:

Yes, my dearest children, I do want to share my deep heart with you and the many who come thirsty for life. Call to their spirits within and invite them into my love! Say simply, "Rise Up and walk," and then breathe this gift of life you have received over the aching heart. Already, you know the capacity of my love and yearn to share it. That is OUR yearning! The Father's and Mine, the Holy Spirit is burning within you. Yes, fire is burning, the torch is lit, and you bear my image. Be regal yet humble in bearing; never diminish my power with feeble excuses. Ask, and it will be given; speak, and it will be done as the Father wills within your temple.

You have many questions about your future, your work, and your assignment in my kingdom. And it is right to say it is not completed. My harvest is ripe, and I will not let it rot in the fields because some will fail to speak my truth. So others will breathe the life that brings them to maturity, and then the harvest can begin. Your doing in this, is my doing. When you are there, I will speak and show up the next need. Do not grow weary. Allow my spirit to refresh you. Come to the water, my well.

As the wind blows, so comes my Spirit, and the chimes play a song of celebration.

Rejoice...REJOICE!

We are born again today in new hearts of healing believers.

REJOICE, because some have died to self and removed the world from their view.
Now they see ME, and I am born anew.
I come, and ANGELS rejoice!
There is joy in the dying and great Glory
In the Resurrection of My saints again.
Fear not, my children. You have kept your covenant; I will keep mine. I will never forsake you! I will cover

you in my shelter—the rocky cleft will hide you far above the battleground below. An eagle's nest will not be seen, nor arrows pierce the ground you stand upon.

Amen, so let it be.

Reflections

These questions are meant to encourage you to think about this subject and share in discussion with others.

1. What would most of us conclude from witnessing the desperate struggles within our world to reach a consensus about what is acceptable moral behavior?
2. How do we administer justice while building a society that respects the rights of every "outgroup"?
3. Have societies' "outgroups" become self-appointed "righteous and holy people"?
4. Do you think that every effort that's begun soon degenerates into some kind of entity, policy, organization, or movement that hurts people?
5. Do we have a society, a media, and an elitist culture that is overwhelmed by popular cultural pressure?

For your own personal reflection:

1. Has there been a time in your life when moral ambiguity became a personal swamp?
2. Have you felt personally pressured by popular beliefs in your personal life or any organization?
3. Do you trust the depth of your relationship with the Lord so that you can walk in righteousness?

Guidepost V

Suffering

Introduction

I ask you to prayerfully absorb this powerful word from the Lord... believe me; I could not write this myself! And notice how He tells us that, as highlighted below, that wisdom and power will not grow in soil untouched by 1) His Spirit, 2) His righteousness and purity, 3) His sacrificial presence, and 4) His healing. These are things you must gain in your spiritual journey up to Jerusalem, and so, we arrive at Guidepost V after having looked into those topics.

*This is the **fifth Guidepost** on your return to Holiness, Virgin Israel, My people, and My righteous ones. It is suffering because not one person is holy, just, and righteous at birth but rather enters into a body that will be corrupted and a soul divided from its source and its Savior at birth. You have entered into My testing, My trying, My discipline, My identity fulfilled in suffering and through the Way of the Cross ordained for Me and by Me. You must traverse this* *heavy atmosphere, where decay, death, and disease combine with the perverted power of the evil one to contain you in suffering. To recognize these devices and conditions and command my Authority over them is wisdom.* **This wisdom and power will not grow in soil untouched by my Spirit, my righteousness and purity preceded by my sacrificial presence and healing.** *All these building blocks together have laid out the gateway to suffering. You have asked to know the fellowship of sharing in my suffering and the power of my resurrection. Because you want to know me, you must know the wisdom of suffering.*

My people have turned their backs on me when mankind succumbed to the power of the evil one and unbelievable suffering pursued them. Some, but not all. Is suffering the tragic loss of a beloved child or the vicious attack upon a mother by her own child? There is no measure and no definition. It is amorphous, ever-changing, as the enemy tries to win souls to hopelessness!

The above words were written on May 4, 2017, following two incredible pieces of our Jerusalem tour. The first was our brief but emotional sojourn in the pit-like jail that was likely where our Lord was held overnight between His arrest, examination by the Jews, and eventual condemnation to death through Pontius Pilate. We listened to the words of Psalm 88, which our Lord no doubt knew by heart and could have spoken in that place. As you read this slowly, imagine a dark, dank, and deep circular stone pit, at least 20 feet deep, with a small hole at the top through which the prisoner was lowered. His heart was heavy, his hands still bleeding from the garden; he is weeping...

[1] Lord, you are the God who saves me; day and night I cry out to you.

[2] May my prayer come before you; turn your ear to my cry.

[3] I am overwhelmed with trouble and my life draws near to death.

[4] I am counted among those who go down to the pit; I am like one without strength.

[5] I am set apart with the dead, like the slain who lie in the grave, whom you remember no more, who are cut off from your care.

[6] You have put me in the lowest pit, in the darkest depths.

[7] Your wrath lies heavily on me; you have overwhelmed me with all your waves.

[8] You have taken from me my closest friends and have made me repulsive to them.

I am confined and cannot escape;

[9] my eyes are dim with grief. I call to you, Lord, every day; I spread out my hands to you.

[14] Why, Lord, do you reject me and hide your face from me?

[15] From my youth I have suffered and been close to death; I have borne your terrors and am in despair.

None of us who stood there that day at the bottom of the pit were able to keep from crying and sobbing even as we connected with the torturous pain of our Lord.

And then we went to the Holocaust Museum. I do not even have the strength to remember how I stumbled through the museum, attempting to absorb and yet not absorb everything that was on display there. As a student of that history, much of it was familiar to me. But to view the scenes from the ghettos and the camps and see names and faces attached to each tragic moment was devastating. Can anyone not return to a quiet place at the end of such a day and plead before the Lord, "Give us understanding, oh Mighty God! Why are we here? What is going on? What will happen to us? Where are you, Lord?"

I began this portion of the Guidepost with the word the Lord gave me soon after this day. And what follows is my understanding, as minuscule as it is, of how the Word leads us to understand suffering.

Growing through the Grief and Pain of Life's Trials

I shared the testimony of the loss of my son earlier as I wrote about sacrifice, so I will not repeat it here but will add a little more to it shortly. However, it is important to me that you hear that God led me to that understanding of loss transmutated into sacrifice because it is one facet of how we may be led to walk through suffering. It is certainly not the only way in which we understand suffering.

I recently picked up Lee Strobel's book, "The Case for Faith," written from an investigative reporter's perspective in search of the reasons one should put faith in God and specifically in Jesus Christ, the Son of God. Glancing at the chapter headings, I read:

- "A loving God would never torture people in Hell."
- "Since Evil and Suffering Exists, a Loving God cannot"
- "God isn't worthy of Worship if He kills Innocent Children."

Incredibly, Strobel does a remarkably effective job at answering these questions, and I, for one, am grateful that he attempts it. He interviews a man by the name of Peter John Kreeft, Ph.D., who is a Catholic philosopher, has published over 40 books, and is as able as any man alive to answer why evil and suffering exists. In the end, he tells Strobel that the answer to suffering is not an answer at all, *"It's the Answerer. It's Jesus himself. It's not a bunch of words; it's the Word. It's not a tightly woven philosophical argument; it's a person. The person. The answer cannot be an abstract issue; it's a personal issue. Jesus is sitting there, sitting beside us in the lowest places of our lives. Are we broken? He was broken, like bread, for us. Are we despised? He was despised and rejected of men..." "But he (God) knew that Jesus was more than an explanation," He's what we really need. If your friend is sick and dying, the most important thing he wants is not an explanation; he wants you to sit with him! He's terrified of being alone more than anything else. So, God has not left us alone." And, said Kreeft, "For that I love him." (The Case for Faith, p 52.)*

I have to agree with Peter John Kreeft. Yes, we long for the compassion of God to draw us into union with Him in our suffering. But the scripture quoted earlier, "I want to know Christ and the fellowship of his suffering..." implies something more to me. The following is a word of truth impressed upon me by His Spirit one evening:

My Glory comes in the Sacrificial Death of my only Son. A pain so deep, a well-spring eternal of My tears necessary to wash the sins of my beloved children from their souls so we could be reunited once more, now pours forth. This is everything a Father has to give.

The fellowship of His suffering is attained in the heart of Grief that is washed with the passionate JOY of communion eternal! Receive the gift of faith as a treasure closely guarded in me and not relinquished without forethought to my children.

When one walks in faith through that valley (through the grief of loss), trusting my Son, again, the well-spring of tears that wash away sin is renewed. Because in faith met with sacrifice, I birth mercy, grace, all compassion, and forgiveness. Nothing evil can stand before such a Heart as this.

April 5, 2017

Some Testimony

This perspective from the Father's heart was and is a new revelation to me. We often talk of the sacrifice that Jesus made and the blood He shed to purify us from all sin, but do we ever consider the sacrifice of God the Father? Did you catch the words "This is everything a Father has to give"? Can you imagine the anguish He felt as He watched His only son tortured to death, knowing He had ordained it? And understand the urgent and tragic necessity the Father felt to bring the ultimate sacrifice to fruition for us? I can imagine it only because of my own suffering when I watched my young son meet his death and wept that heart-wrenching flood of tears day after day for many months and even years. God's faithfulness and love bore me up and prevented me from carrying out any of the suicidal impulses that assaulted me. I can remember such sadness and loneliness for my son overwhelming me as I sat and looked at the flooded river rushing by near my home that I wanted to drive me and my car into it! My longing to go to my son was that powerful. He forbade me to do it with the sweet knowledge that I would have another baby soon. I didn't know then that I was pregnant, but I was and soon had an early-term miscarriage. Another grief. But true to His word, I conceived again within two months and had my precious daughter in due time. A few years later, God blessed us with another son as well. What an amazing joy that was!

My Own Exodus

Someone will be asking God and wondering how a good and gracious Father can allow such a pattern of death and grievous loss into someone's life like mine. Death by suicide with infanticide, an early grave due to cancer, abortion, tragic accidents... What possible good can come of it? I recently have been led to study the exodus of the Hebrew people out of Egypt. In that study, the Lord has shown me that I have experienced my own exodus out of slavery, as we all do, complete with plagues. Those events in my early life represented the plagues of blood and the deaths of the firstborn. As difficult as it may be to comprehend that powerful analogy, it has great meaning and even comfort for me. I know that the Lord never took His eyes off me throughout all those years, and He even cried with me. But He knew what He was working into me and out of me with each loss. And, ultimately, I became His servant, as dead to self as He allows and I know how to be, and alive to Him in joy and Redemptive Love.

He gave me His sustenance in my grief and, in that experience, the gift of compassion for God's own suffering. And in my grief, He led me to this scripture:

> [6] In all this you greatly rejoice, though now for a little while you may have had to suffer grief in all kinds of trials. [7] These have come so that the proven genuineness of your faith—of greater worth than gold, which perishes even though refined by fire—may result in praise, glory and honor when Jesus Christ is revealed. [1 Peter 1:6-7 NIV]

A Lesson from Scripture

And yet I know that all of us, as we walk through lonesome valleys, must spend hours and hours in deep communion with our Father in Heaven and carefully study the scriptures to come into this place which passes all understanding, even when faced with the deepest suffering we can imagine. God will give that to you. I can share my story, but He alone is the giver of truth you can internalize and make your own. Now, however, in order to share what has been most meaningful for me in my walk through the trials of life without a complete theological treatise, I must begin with some biblically sound beliefs. What I believe is:

1. We have and serve a sovereign God. He is righteous, holy, and just, and He has a plan and an agenda that will bring all things into His divine order for the universe under the headship of Christ, in His time.
2. We also contend with the presence of evil in this universe, which is powerful and very personal in his attempts to thwart the Father's just, holy, and worthy intentions.
3. God allowed this condition to develop on the earth for His purposes, and we must accept that His ways are above our ways and that we cannot fathom the depth and complexity of His thoughts. Rather, we must, in faith, believe that *"God works all things together for good for those who love him and are called according to his purposes"* (Rom 8:28).
4. The highest fulfillment of our purpose on earth is to glorify God (Matt 5:16; Col 3:17; John 117:4).

Let us make very clear our position in regard to our Savior and the evil one who rules over the earth. 1 John 5:19 states, *"We know that we are children of God and that the whole world is under the control of the evil one."* Also, we know that we are *"in him who is true-even in his son Jesus Christ"* (1 John 5:20). So, we must test our commitment to our Lord Jesus and see if the depth of that desire in us to serve Him corresponds to the cost He paid for our salvation. We have been bought at the cost of His life, His body broken, and blood spilled for us. We do not have any personal right to our lives if we are His bondservants. In fact, Jesus bought and <u>paid for us</u>; otherwise, we would belong to Satan and would be bound for hell. This is the Holy exchange that we have made, and our commitment must include the recognition that, as Jesus told us, *"The world will hate us, as it hated him* (John 15:18). Remember that the world is under Satan's control, and Satan hates Jesus because He alone has broken his rule over death. Therefore, Satan will hate us as well.

I believe that Jesus was deadly serious when He said, *"If any man comes to me and hate not his father, mother, wife, children, brothers, sisters and yes, even his own life, he cannot be my disciple. And who ever does not bear his cross and come after me, cannot be my disciple"* (Luke 14:26-27). Remember that this was said within a culture that spoke in hyperbole to make a point. "Hate" meant to "love less" or regard others as second to one's Lord. It is important that bearing one's cross is the condition of discipleship. And that follows upon the emotional or actual separation from family, which was always the most important institution of the Jewish culture and the model for our caring for one another in love. I note that the Lord did not include husbands and wives in this list. I believe that was because marriage, the covenant relationship, is the most intimate of all and foreshadows the deeper intimacy to come in our lives with the indwelling of the Holy Spirit that Jesus would send to us upon His death. Our Lord confirms this with His many references to Himself as the Bridegroom and we, His church, as His Bride.

Is it any surprise that the Apostle Paul tells us in no uncertain terms that *"since you have been raised with Christ, set your hearts on things above... For you died, and your life is now hidden with Christ in God. When Christ, who is your life, appears, then you also will appear with him in glory"?* (Col. 3: 1-4)

Yes, this dying to the old nature and our old allegiances brings with it the promise of being *"renewed in knowledge in the image of its Creator" as we "put on the new self,"* but doesn't it also echo Jesus' warning that we must *"bear our cross and come after me"?* Put simply, the CROSS is an instrument of death—death to all of our worldly desires, the flesh nature, the normal human wants, needs, and comforts. We may not necessarily lose all those things in this life. In fact, we may be materially blessed and have a life full of the joys of this world. But we are called to embrace dying to this world and living in Christ, **"who is our life."**

Suffering: God's Perspective

Suffering, in the light of God's perspective, takes on a much different meaning and implication. If I choose to believe His truth for me that *"I have been crucified with Christ and I no longer live, but Christ lives in me. The life I now live in the body, I live by faith in the Son of God, who loved me and gave himself for me"* (Gal 2:20), then I have no fear of any loss, any trial or persecution that the evil one may devise against me or that God might allow to try and test me. The rest of Gal 2:20 is *"I do not set aside the grace of God, for if righteousness could be gained through the law, Christ died for nothing."* But the cross in my life is both voluntary and involuntary loss. It is a symbol of the path I walk toward the righteousness already given by God. We cannot claim immunity to death, disease, tragedies, and the normal trials of life based on our standing in Christ and being under His Lordship. Jesus famously told us in Matt. 5:44, " *But I tell you, love your enemies and pray for those who persecute you, 45-that you may be children of your Father in heaven. He causes his sun to rise on the evil and the good and sends rain on the righteous and the unrighteous.*"

In other words, do the impossible! Love your enemies and pray for your persecutors; be as righteous as possible, and you will be the Father's children, <u>but</u> do not in any way associate rewards from God as a result of your attempt at righteousness! God is Sovereign, and of the trials He has allowed to come to man, Jesus once said, *"But this happened <u>so that</u> the works of God might be displayed in him"* (John 9:3). The Apostle Paul says, *"We were under great pressure, far beyond our ability to endure, so that we despaired of life itself. ⁹ Indeed, we felt we had received the sentence of death. <u>But this happened that we might not rely on ourselves but on God</u>, who raises the dead"* (2 Cor. 1:8). The lesson in this is that God will be glorified in the trials we endure and that we will LEARN to depend on God and Him alone. That sounds so simple, doesn't it? Why do we continue to question the Lord when evil overwhelms us?

Jesus said in John 16:7-12 that He would send the Holy Spirit, the Counselor, to us and *"when he comes he will convict the world of guilt in regard to sin and righteousness and judgment: ...and about judgment because the prince of this world now stands condemned."* Alright, we say, this is Satan's position: he, the evil one, is condemned; we know that the power of death has been broken because Jesus has conquered death, and yet scripture tells us that (even though) *"We know we are from God, the whole world is under the control of the evil one"* (1 John 5:19). What are we to make of this? We learn in various scriptures, which will be covered in detail in another chapter, that Satan can be told to "Get behind me" just as Jesus did, and he can be rebuked and ordered to leave someone or someplace. Yet, Satan has a "legal" right to continue his attempts to win us over to "his side" throughout our lives! Living with suffering is just plain difficult, so how do I reconcile this paradox of scripture? I look at how the evil one continues doing his work and recognize that "he stands condemned," and I believe that he feels that condemnation…

- Every time a confession of faith is made and a child of God receives salvation
- Every time a spiritual bondage is broken
- Every time a healing happens
- Every time a saint escapes the bonds of sickness and death and goes to heaven
- Every time lives are resurrected from the bondages of sin, Satan, self, the world, and religion
- Every time love is returned for hatred
- Every time forgiveness is given for transgression.
- Every time God is Glorified!

I am reassured as I witness the truth of all these above statements, and as I grow in my own intimacy with God and my dependence on Him each day, I learn to withstand the "body blows" to my heart as dear friends and family receive terminal diagnoses of cancer—twice this week. Even as hurricanes bring devastation to millions, Russia makes war unjustly, HAMAS sends terrorists into Israel, forest fires burn out of control, and mad men threaten nuclear war, I stand firm in His love and my knowledge of and faith in my Redeemer, Yeshua.

A Testimony

I recently deleted a relevant testimony here about the trials of marriage as I confronted again a real and very painful source of suffering in my life and the lives of thousands around the world: suicide.

Recently, there was a suicide of an adolescent daughter of a family deeply devoted to God and to family ministry. In the immediate wake of that loss, a dear friend of that family said to me that she felt such a burden for the pain that the siblings left behind would be feeling. At that, I stopped in my busy tracks, sat down, and cried—deep, angry, gushing tears. I felt angry at God and let out my frustration toward Him; yes, He can take it and wants to hear it all. I wept as I asked, "Where are you GOD?? Why does this happen? And who was there for us to explain and pick up the pieces in the wake of my own sister's suicide, which also took the life of her unborn child? Where was the church, the love of God, the compassion?" My experience at the time of her death was that of sinking into a deep chasm of shame, in total isolation from family, church, and friends. I remember saying to one friend who ventured an "I'm sorry about your sister," "That's ok, we weren't really that close anyway." Lies, denial, shame, and pain. I began then to stuff down those real emotions and carry instead a shield of anger. It was 4 or 5 years before I began to put aside that shield and pick up something closer to loving-kindness.

In the news, two very well-known celebrities died by their own hands in apparent suicides. And the news reports a 25-30% increase in our nation's rate of suicide since 1999. I cannot here address all the causes of depression and despair or address the partially known remedies. But those who LOVE GOD and are called according to His purposes, as I have been, learn to put all events, all suffering squarely on the very broad shoulders of our Lord, who has pledged to bear our burdens. Then I looked at these events and my scriptural beliefs again and listened for a word from the Father, He who has said that He "works all things together for our good" (Rom 8:28). Here is what I heard:

You've confessed your anger; now repent, release control, and be obedient to MY Way, Truth, and Life. No more! Be patient; the wolves have been released. Like hungry lions, they devour the piety of all my righteous ones. The child (the victim of suicide) is with me from the beginning. He (the evil one) cannot have the innocent victims of suicide. But the vain pietous believer Satan will devour until I hear their confession and forgive.

This is a hard Word to receive when we are the ones guilty of that false piety. We count on our piety to protect us from the evil in this world and then get angry at God and reject Him when things don't work out according to our own sense of what is righteous and holy for the children of God. Clearly, said the Lord in the above message, He is working the tares out of our character in every occurrence.

This, then, is what I think the Father would say to all of us:

I am Your God; there is only One of ME, I am the Alpha and Omega, the Beginning... and End and, I AM Love. I yearn to know and love each of you intimately! To connect you to My source of Eternal Love and Power. A place of quiet safety...My all-sufficient place is like a mother's womb; you need never leave, timeless and nurturing. Be in ME, and all your pain, anger, hatred, frustration, self-seeking, and striving will disappear. There is enough for all. Come...I will never run out.

LOVE- Abba Father

In the end, I choose to say with Paul, *"I want to know Christ—yes, to know the power of his resurrection and <u>participation in his sufferings</u>, becoming like him in his death, [11] and so, somehow, attaining to the resurrection from the dead"* (Phil 3:10-11), or say nothing at all and live this life out on my own, in half-hearted Christianity that despairs but "hopes for the best." That is not an option I have ever wanted to contemplate because, throughout my life, the Lord has repeatedly exposed me to His knowledge of *"the prize for which God has called me heavenward in Christ Jesus"* (Phil 3:14) *and the "peace of God which transcends all understanding <u>does</u> guard my heart and mind in Jesus"* (Phil 3:7). This is just the beginning of the passion with which I choose Christ over chaos, over darkness...over evil.

Your Key For the Journey: THIS HAPPENED SO THAT....

Wherever the Lord has placed you in service to Him, you will participate in His sufferings through your own personal life and the fellowship of sharing in the suffering of all His children. He has given all of us this word of reassurance:

In my wisdom, you will hear the source of all pain in the lost and those who hunger for fellowship with me yet are locked outside the gate. You will open the gate so that they may pass through. For in my death, all sorrow, evil, and sin are washed away. My death is the source of forgiveness, which is the healing balm for all wounds. It is transformational. Forgive them as I have forgiven you, by the Cross, which means "I bear your suffering for you."

Your Lord, Yeshua

Reflections

Suffering is very difficult and extremely personal. As I confess, self-pity kept suffering hidden in me. What emotions are you feeling right now? I pray you have a group of friends around you that you can share those feelings with.

1. What seems to sustain you now when you face difficult times? Is it your favorite person to talk with and mull things over, or is it your comfy chair and a cuppa? Maybe it's something stronger? Something potentially addictive?
2. How do you think you can make the switch from the usual way of life and coping to a Christ-centered and focused way? Perhaps you feel like you have done so already. Think about how you did that.
3. Which scriptures have you memorized so well that they really pop into your mind readily? List a few.
4. Our objective in this book is to have the Mind of Christ. What does that mean to you?

Guidepost VI

His Promises are True: Hope Produces Courage and Perseverance

Why are we just now being led to study the Promises of God and the hope that produces courage and perseverance? Discipleship is truthfully a lifelong process in which we build our faith temples to God one brick at a time. Sometimes, a huge production of those bricks can stymie our personal progress and leave us inundated as we dig out from under some tremendous grief or an illness that redirects our path. But just imagine the greatest promises Jesus gave to His disciples and when they were spoken! After His resurrection, He told them they must wait 40 days for the Holy Spirit to come. The night before He died, He told them that it was better that He leave them so that the Holy Spirit would come. In His last days on earth, He promised that though He was going to die, He would rise again in three days. He saved all the big stuff for last. Jesus knew the pace at which His disciples could absorb the life-changing reality that being a follower of Jesus would bring. And so, after facing the truths of sacrifice and suffering, the reality of our righteousness being placed firmly in God's hands, as well as any healing we receive, and the gracious beginning of the new Covenant, we come to this joyous fact: what Jesus has promised, HE WILL DO.

Shiloh, Israel: Where Hope Produces Courage and Perseverance

At the site of the first tabernacle in Shiloh, where the Glory of the Lord God rested for 369 years on His people, Israel, Hannah prayed to the Lord directly, just quietly speaking under her breath, the first time a woman ever openly approached the Lord in His temple. She prayed to the Lord that He would grant her a child. Our archeologist guide, a lovely woman of conservative Jewish tradition, shared with us that this site is a place still imbued with the Spirit of God, where prayers for miracles are answered regularly. Women who have been infertile pray for the blessing of a child, and God answers those prayers. She gets emails full of joy and thanksgiving often. She believes it is because of Hannah's bold prayer and the answer from God that gave her son, the prophet Samuel, to the nation of Israel.

In this holy atmosphere during our time of deep prayer, I heard the promises of God for my own children as I cried out to Him and was reminded of my own promise: to dedicate them to the Lord, raise them in the knowledge of the Lord, and release them again into His great purposes. My children are wonderful young adults, and they are currently "writing their testimonies" as they walk in the ways of the world. That's ok. I am fine with waiting, knowing how long it took my Lord to completely wake me up to His glory, His hope, and His promises.

But...can I even explain from my own experience what it means to have received the **hope**—in other words, the

belief—that my children are known to God, who has a plan for them? He gave me very clear and specific words for each child that I will never forget, although they each face life-threatening and life-altering circumstances. My mother's heart would have been crushed already seeing what they had gone through. But I know the end of the story! This is the **PERSEVERENCE** that we are promised.

As always, I am reminded by my loving God: *"For I know the plans I have for You, declares the Lord, plans to prosper and not to harm you, plans to give you Hope and a future."* But do we know the rest of this scripture? It is imperative that we do because God says, *"'THEN you will seek me and find me when you seek me with all your heart. I will be found by you,' declares the Lord!"* (! added) (Jer 29:11-14). He is anxious to be found by YOU. God is not hiding from you, playing cat and mouse, or making everything a guessing game. You need **only** *"seek first his kingdom and his righteousness, and all these things will be added unto you!"* (Matt 6:33). Jesus knew the promises of His Father that He came to fulfill.

When given such glorious, good news, I want to break into song and worship the Lord:

The Light of the world who came down into darkness,
opened my eyes (to) let me see!
Beauty that makes this heart adore you,
all for a life lived in thee:
Here I am to worship,
Here I am to bow down,
Here I am to say that you're my God.[7]

As I listened to my Abba Father, He whispered:

Hearts now rejoice entwined and beat as one. Mine and yours, says the Father! A Place where darkness

---

7   Here I Am to Worship, lyrics by Darlene Zschech, Tim Hughes

cannot penetrate nor exist. There I am in you, and you rest in me, above all you see, and my breath is in all you feel and think. BE, simply be....

You may hold the Holy worship of MY word within you. Those sounds that I spoke to create life are Words of Life. Speak, think, feel <u>life</u> for all you meet, for this is their true condition. Death and darkness is the deceiver who attempts to cover over life. He IS defeated in My Name. My Kaddish light causes his particulate to disperse, and he is shattered by my holy light. Feed the flame that has been lit in you.

Lessons from First Samuel

There is a powerful lesson on the impact of the promises of God in 1 Samuel 28. You may want to open the word to this chapter and read it all or follow along. In this chapter, Saul, having expelled all of the witches and mediums from the land in an attempt to regain his righteousness, goes in disguise to the Witch of Endor. He has found himself in a very weak position because God has cut him off, and he has her call up the deceased prophet Samuel. He learns from Samuel that what the Lord had said He would do was about to happen because Saul did not obey the Lord in carrying out His fierce wrath against the Amalekites (vs18); so, the Lord will now hand over Israel and Saul and his sons to the Philistines. Tomorrow, "you and your sons will be with me," says Samuel. "Immediately, Saul fell full length on the ground, filled with fear because of Samuel's words," the next verse tells us. Saul has been disobedient and is about to experience the full measure of God's anger and disappointment with him. God's promises are true, but Saul has no hope.

Yet, we should not miss the point that as Saul exits this earth, he is given a promise from the greatest Prophet in the land, Samuel (even though recently deceased), that he would be *"with him tomorrow."* Pause...

Now David, who had been given the kingdom when it was "torn out of your [Saul's] hands" (1 Sam 28:17) was sent home by the Philistines to Ziklag, preventing him from going to war against Saul and the Israelites. (Long story short, they had a falling out, and David lived a year amongst the Philistines). But in his absence, God allowed David's home to be raided by the Amalekites, those same bad actors that Saul had failed to take out of the picture. David found his own home was burned, and every person taken captive, and David and his men wept aloud until they had no strength left to weep (1 Sam 30:4). Yet *"David found strength in the Lord his God"*! (1 Sam 30:6) God promises David that he should pursue the Amalekites and *"You will certainly overtake them and succeed in the rescue"* (1 Sam 30:8). David, in strict obedience, pursues the promises of God, succeeds, and brings home all those taken captive, his wives and sons included, and lots of plunder.

Promises believed and hope in the Lord produced the courage to persevere.

Meanwhile, Saul and the Israelites go to war with the Philistines. The battle has turned against Saul; his sons are slain, and he is critically wounded. He seeks death at the hand of his armor-bearer, who, terrified, refuses to do it, so he falls on his own sword. *"So Saul and his three sons and his armor-bearer and all his men died together that same day."* (1 Sam 31:6).

At first, I believed that this was a story about Saul's hope lost and the failed courage of a displaced king who ended his life in suicide. However, I believe that even though it ended badly, God's promises are true. Knowing that he was assured of losing the battle as well as the kingdom to David, **Saul clung to the final promise of God, given through Samuel, to be in a place they knew only as Sheol, with Samuel that day, and embraced death bravely when the end came.** Oddly, his suicide was based on that hope, which Saul had already established in the eternal God of the universe, and *that hope produced the courage to carry out his last act on earth*. This type of death was considered honorable at the time when Samuel, David, and Saul lived. Somewhere in heaven, Samuel and Saul are reliving this and, I believe, rejoicing that the God-given lessons of their time on Earth are still being scribed and taught to every generation.

Hope: Another Dimension

This other dimension is obedience to God's commands and His discipline of us when we stray.

I have shared my own very real story of hope based on the belief that God's promises are true and the illustrations from scripture. From the first promise God made to Abraham to make of his seed a great nation, God's promises have been spoken into reality. And yet, in our humanness, we push back against the lesson of Saul's life in particular and wonder how an act of suicide can ever be allowed by a good God. If, in fact, the prophetic announcement by Samuel from beyond the grave was the precursor to God's discipline, then accepting it led Saul to his culturally noble act of suicide.

The writer of Hebrews helps us understand that God disciplines His sons and, quoting Proverbs 3:11-12, says:

"My son, do not make light of the Lord's discipline, and **do not lose heart when he rebukes you,** [6] **because the Lord**

disciplines the one he loves, and he chastens everyone he accepts as his son."

[7]Endure hardship as discipline; God is treating you as his children. For what children are not disciplined by their father? [8] If you are not disciplined—and everyone undergoes discipline—then you are not legitimate, not true sons and daughters at all. [9]Moreover, we have all had human fathers who disciplined us and we respected them for it. How much more should we submit to the Father of our spirits and live! [10] For a short time they disciplined us as they thought best, but God does it for our good, so that we may share in his holiness. [11]No discipline seems pleasant at the time, but painful. Later on, however, for those who have been trained by it, it produces a harvest of righteousness and peace. [Heb 12:5-11]

We must learn to accept that discipline is ultimately good and comes from the Father! It is given to us "so that we may share in his holiness," the scripture says. Is that not equivalent to seeing God's hopes and plans fulfilled? However, discipline is not punishment. When we discipline our children, for example, we do it out of love and in order for them to grow in righteous thinking and behavior. Punishment, however, is meted out without careful thought and results in feelings of shame and condemnation. While God may judge us and even condemn our sin, He never intends to shame us. Shame, I believe, is Satan's tool of destruction and really does great harm to the human spirit. We know that this is not God's action because, in Psalm 34:5, we learn that "Those who look to Him are radiant; their faces are never covered with shame." Discipline eventually purifies us from evil and produces the fruit of righteousness or "right standing with God."

Are you a stubborn, rebellious child who keeps reaching into the fire, convinced that your Father wouldn't have left it there if it were truly dangerous? Do you believe He wouldn't have made it so attractive, enticing, or seemingly delicious if it were actually harmful to your health, righteousness, and peace? Do you keep touching or consuming it, thinking it won't hurt you again?

The common denominator in discipline and punishment is that they both can be painful. The pain has a different quality to it, however. I think I can liken the discipline of God to that pain I feel when my physical therapist is working loose a frozen joint. It's a pain that is usually a good stretch with a sharp point or two. Sometimes, discipline is a much longer-lasting experience and requires digging deep into the wells of trust and patience, deep breathing through the intense hard times, and forced resting in the Father's care without conscious effort. The end result is greater wisdom and the awareness that He is very present with us. Punishment, on the other hand, just feels painful and unjust, causing confused and angry feelings, even if we know the logic behind it and agree with it in principle. It sometimes "teaches a lesson" and sometimes is a wasted effort from which no one learns.

His Promises

What, then, are we to make of all this discipline if God's promises are true?

> At that time his voice shook the earth, but now he has promised, "Once more I will shake not only the earth but also heaven." [27] The expression "once more" signifies the removal of what can be shaken, that is, created things, so that what cannot be shaken may remain. Hebrews 12:26-27

What Cannot be Shaken?

[28] Therefore, since we are receiving a kingdom that cannot be shaken, let us be thankful, and so worship God acceptably with reverence and awe, [29] for our "God is a consuming fire." vs. 28-29

We who walk in that kingdom now know that the cornerstone is Jesus Christ, and His principles for our unshakable kingdom are faith, hope, and love. *"And now these three remain; faith, hope and love. But the greatest of these is love"* (1 Cor 13:13).

This unshakable kingdom we are being given is built upon the supremacy of Christ. This is the theme in chapter 1 of Colossians: "He is the image of the invisible God, the first-born over all creation, For by him all things were created." You likely know the powerful truths of who Christ was, is, and is to be, but what does that mean for us? Look at verses 19-20. It's the reconciliation of all things to God that impacts our identity in Christ, our present, and our future. How have we been reconciled, and what does that mean?

> Once you were alienated from God and were enemies in your minds because of your evil behavior. But now he has reconciled you by Christ's physical body through death to present you holy in his sight, without blemish and free from accusation— if you continue in your faith, established and firm, and do not move from the hope held out in the gospel. Col 1:21-23

THAT'S LOVE, FAITH AND HOPE,

And you are:

- Reconciled through His death (ultimate sacrificial **love**) to make you holy in His sight.
- Given the choice to continue in your **faith**. Some do not; some do turn away when it gets difficult. Will you?
- Encouraged to not move from the **hope**. This means you can move away from hope. How, when, where, why, and will any of us succumb? We are not meant to fear losing our salvation, losing our faith, and losing hope, but we are meant to be careful and

watchful over this tremendous gift we have been given and to keep our lamps lit!

My Hope is in Christ, and His promises for me and my children are true.

Col 2:13-15 assures me that:

1. I am alive with Christ!
2. I am forgiven!
3. I am armed!

He disarmed the powers and the authorities! Because of the work already done in Christ, because He did it in the heavenlies, I can step into the authority given me and persevere!

Now What? Perseverance

So then, just as you received Christ Jesus as Lord, <u>continue to live your lives in him,</u> [7]rooted and built up in him, strengthened in the faith as you were taught, and overflowing with thankfulness. Col 2: 6-7

This is your job, **to continue.** It is not a done thing; it requires your work and commitment to be rooted and built because you are still in that state of fallen-ness, and you must:

<u>Set your mind</u> on things above, not on earthly things. [3] For you died, and your life is now hidden with Christ in God. Col 3:2-3

Again, this is an activity that <u>you must be open to.</u> However, in the Greek, the word meaning "set the mind" is *phren*, used in the passive imperative tense (Strongs NT 5426). Scholars have assured me that this means God expects me to be the passive, still, or quiet recipient of His power to act. If I can accept this truth, He is the one who will take me mentally to that place where I am hidden with Christ in God. Although, since your salvation and deliverance from oppression, it seems to have become easier to change your mind about life and turn to God, He is the only one with the power to captivate our minds and spirits for eternity and keep us there with Him.

> But now <u>you must also rid</u> yourselves of all such things as these: anger, rage, malice, slander, and filthy language from your lips. [9] Do not lie to each other, since you have <u>taken off</u> your old self with its practices [10] and have <u>put on</u> the new self, which is <u>being renewed</u> in knowledge in the image of its Creator. Col 3:8

➢ What we must do is walk it out, walk in freedom, and recognize when we have fallen again into the slime pit of life that we now **"must also rid"** ourselves of those things that pollute our lives. Repent and be forgiven.

➢ What God has done by His Holy Spirit is provided the new self which **you have put on**, which is **being renewed** in knowledge in the image of your Creator. This is God's creative action. He alone provides the knowledge and the image of Himself to us. This last point is important:

➢ Understand that what God has done for you in the provision of your new self cannot remain if it is taken off daily and hung in the closet with last year's suit. Don't go out naked into this wicked world. It requires **your active daily participation to put on, to cleanse, and to renew it**.

You must do it! Don't send it out to the cleaners once a week or a month and think that it's good enough. It's too fragile and will disintegrate like any physical body without being put on and exercised daily!

Mini Testimony

This is an example of the passive imperative *phren* that allows God to take me to that place where, hidden in Christ, my behavior can be changed by Him.

Have you ever chugged along slowly and patiently behind a car towing a large trailer of farm equipment, waiting your turn on that narrow country road until the broken lines allow passing, only to have the car behind you zoom out, almost hitting the first guy and you, so he could be on his merry way? If you are like me, this makes you very mad; there may be angry words and gestures flying, but...that's not very Christian now, is it? So today, I chose to let God in and surrender to His wise mind, knowing He would rid me of this angry and ugly behavior. "Surely," I said to myself, "I was justified; that other guy was driving dangerously and was inconsiderate. Shouldn't we all follow the same rules of the road?" That's my belief. My thought was, *You stupid a..., You could've killed me!* The feeling was anger and vengeance, even. Yuck!

I knew, as God's wise mind counselor, that I had to change that belief somehow. And I did this by addressing the source of chaos, danger, and all evil actions. The other driver's selfishness and recklessness were driven by a spirit of chaos, either in him or the atmosphere, and that spirit was what needed to be addressed. I have been given God's power to do so because we battle not against "flesh and blood but the powers and principalities of the evil one." Finally, then, what I will do is pray and declare my protection from these forces of chaos every time I go out, ahead of time, and rebuke them when I see them in action, not the individual who has been taken captive.

The Promise of God to His People Israel

I am the least qualified to address this topic for a whole nation of people—a holy and righteous nation of priests—whom we know were called by God to initiate something on Earth never seen before. And yet, as a grafted-in Christian member of that nation, it has weighed on my heart to see the complete unity of believers in the One God come into existence now as we await the return of Yeshua Ha Messiah. Since returning from Israel and witnessing the political disarray, as well as the theological and spiritual divisions of my own Jewish friends and fellow citizens, the Father gave me some understanding of how I have contributed to the division and the gulf that seems to be widening, and what He desired of me.

God's Promises to His People Israel

This Word came based on a Christ-centered understanding of Israel:

My people were called to reverential fear for my statutes. Called out of slavery to build a nation wholly dependent on obedience to me. They feel now that their passion for my law is disrespected or even ridiculed by my Church, the body of Christ, and my heart is grieved so sorely.

I showed you the acts of faith in Hebrews and the deeds my people walked in to understand the depth of their love and desire for me. Out of slavery and into a nation of Priests, they now minister justice to the poor, feed the widows, and nurture the orphans. This is pure and true.

Yet, the wheat and the tares linger, not yet joyful in my coming to return and restore David's glorious kingdom. Join as one with respect to my commandments and rule as one from the heart of Me. Lay aside the arguments and pretenses of literal interpretation until the banquet table is full and the ingathering complete. You can convince some to come in—My people are hungry for pure religion. Then the Exodus will be completed, and they will see with eyes that see and allow Me to come into empty, hungry hearts.

Act in faith, as did your forefathers of the nations. Be taught that all you believe for is possible, and my mind will guide you in all you believe. To the greater awakening of my remnant, my body on earth, I leave this eternal inheritance as a position of authority in which they will advance as chosen and submitted. Be witnesses to pure faith in all humility, knowing only my words, spoken in Spirit to the onlooking critics as well as the souls hungry for truth.

Your actions will repair the tears and the tares of centuries of ill-positioned words. My word, my love, must take its rightful place to rule and to reign in humble authority.

Learn this, daughter. Learn well and restore the things that once were there, first portion, highest seated, in your heart.

It seems that we "Christians" have a critical part to play in the kingdom of Israel to come. We cannot and have not replaced our Hebrew forefathers, as some earlier Christians postulated, but we have discouraged them by our disregard for the faith of our fathers and probably our irreverent contemporary Western lifestyle. We are charged to be convincing witnesses, to testify to the pure faith of the sacrificial love of Messiah in our every thought, word, and deed. Indeed to give a reason for the HOPE we have in Yeshua Ha Messiah.

A Personal Testimony in the Making

I find that, like most of my contemporaries in the faith who have older or adult children, I am in that stage of child development that we call "writing their testimonies." I pray, interceding for them daily, and patiently trust in God's magnificently working out the details. They no longer want to discuss the faith they were raised in, and although it breaks my heart, I am reconciled to that; I respect their boundaries. But the Lord knows no boundaries or limits, and I know He has heard my prayers. Every single one! Here is a beautiful word of assurance that I received from a friend the very day that I sat down to finish writing this chapter, knowing that although God's promises are true, we do not know the day or the hour that He chooses to work them out:

In the spirit, I saw a heavenly rush of angels gathering. Prayers of mothers crying out for their children seemed to have gathered momentum. These prayers, as though being amplified in the spirit, were pounding, relentlessly shaking the door hinges of Heaven. Heaven itself had been shaken by these violent prayers as though a bear had been robbed of its cubs. "Answer the Front Door!"

I heard a loud voice from the throne shout to the angels, "Answer the front door! The 'bowl of prayers for children' prayed by their mothers is now full and tipping over! Angels, receive your assignments!"

I then saw angels stand at attention while the names of these children and their personal addresses were being written on them. Some were "on-the-street addresses" unknown by man but known by God. There were "prison addresses." Even telephone numbers were being given out to some angels who would make person-to-person telephone calls on the earth to some of these children. Some assignments of angels unaware were just to make phone calls and speak to their hearts things nobody else knew. On the streets, pay phones would ring, and homeless children would be led to answer these ringing phones and receive a call from heaven. 'I Am Awakening Your Children and Grandchildren'

The enemy is about to hear from our children and grandchildren, beginning this season. Watch and expect the passion for Christ to run wild like a raging fire inside of them. The Lord has allowed them to be placed in strategic locations on the earth, even in some un-usual places where we think they shouldn't be, held in Satan's grip.

They have now been divinely positioned to become a firebrand in God's hand to ignite and explode like dynamite inside the camp of the enemy! This is why the enemy forever has fought against marriages. He feared concerning the godly seed that was about to come upon the earth to do him in. And here they come!

"Your descendants will defeat their enemies." Gen. 22:17c, MSG

I know His promises and the words of the above pro-phetic word are generally true (although I don't claim to know the specifics of angelic assignments) because the Word says:

"As for me, this is my covenant with them," says the LORD. "My Spirit, who is on you, will not depart from you, and my words that I have put in your mouth will always be on your lips, on the lips of your children and on the lips of their descendants--from this time on and forever," says the LORD. Isa 59:21

...and need I say that "my Spirit" is the Holy Spirit, and "my words" again point us to Jesus Christ, who is **The WORD.**

> They will not labor in vain, nor will they bear children doomed to misfortune; for they will be a people blessed by the LORD, they and their descendants with them. [Isa 65:23]

Our salvation and our children's sealed with the presence of the Holy Spirit in us as a guarantee (2 Cor 5:5) is the mystery of God revealed in Christ the Lord (Col 2:2). I am overwhelmed with the strength and the power in the word of God as He sings His promises like shafts of light into this mother's heart!

Count the Promises of God in this one scripture alone and let your heart soar:

> Therefore, since we have been justified through faith, we have peace with God through our Lord Jesus Christ, [2]through whom we have gained access by faith into this grace in which we now stand. And we boast in the hope of the glory of God.[3]Not only so, but, we also glory in our sufferings because we know that suffering produces perseverance; [4]perseverance, character; and character, hope. [5] And hope does not put us to shame, because God's love has been poured out into our hearts through the Holy Spirit, who has been given to us. [Romans 5:1-5]

I count nine or ten!

Having faith and peace lead us into grace, and the hope of God's Glory is ours. However, when sufferings come, we glory because they lead us back to HOPE that does not put us to shame, because God's love has been poured out into our hearts by the Holy Spirit. When hearts are filled with His love, there is no room ever for shame. Shame is the calling card of the enemy of our souls who seeks to kill and destroy. The Christian has no need to tolerate the lies of shame, even briefly. That "calling card" is a call to warfare: "submit to God, rebuke the devil, and he will flee!" (James 4:7).

Either way, we are assured of our entrance into the hope of the glory of God! Either way!!

Can I get a Hallelujah and sing, "Christ in me, Christ in me, Christ in me the Hope of Glory, You are all I need"?

Early in July, the Spirit of God impressed upon me to write:

There is an order to my universe. Yes, you have learned this, and my intentions and paths are complex yet simply lead to my return. Each heart to their temple, each people to their God, our Father. Each nation to its Holy temple of our Father. Allow the footsteps to stumble until they are made sure by decision and heartfelt commitment to the high road. The return can be difficult, painful even. Treasure these days of grace and seek the paths, each one.

The ancient and holy scripture assures us:

Return to your fortress, O prisoners of hope; even now I announce that I will restore twice as much to you. [Zech 9:12]

Who is your fortress but God alone? "A mighty Fortress is our God, a bulwark never failing!" And who is the cornerstone but Jesus Christ our Lord? And where is the Temple of the Holy Spirit but within each and every one of us purified and made holy?

But those who hope in the Lord will renew their strength. They will soar on wings like eagles. [Isa 40:31]

The Hebrew word for "hope in" or "wait for" is *qavah*, meaning a) to twist or entwine with or b) to continually connect to the Breath of God or revelation of God or Praises to Him....

Selah.

More Testimony

Late Breaking Developments: God is so very faithful that He continues to encourage me with small movements in the hearts and minds of my family. Recently, my husband went to our new church alone, and he told me that he prayed while he was there for our daughter's safety on her trip abroad. This is a huge turnaround and a first step towards the fulfillment of God's promises for our children, as where the father leads, the children will someday walk as well. Father God continues to grow his faith in amazing ways. He is seeing the fruit of our submission, obedience, and hope. He is praying daily for each of our children, and I know and trust that they are feeling this shift in us, as parents, joined together for their ultimate salvation.

Another more amazing thing happened in our family that is so precious and dear to my heart and yet confidential; respect for the family prevents me from speaking. I can say that something was done in the courts of heaven somehow, which attenuated the effects of the courts of man. Someday, this will be shouted from my rooftop with loud Hallelujahs!

God is on the Move!!

Your Key for this Journey: "Get 'er Done" or "Just Do It"! But remember, you are His Holy partner on this earth, and He is the All-Powerful One in all things we do. So get out of His way!

Reflections

1. How does Isaiah 40:31, "Those who hope in the Lord will renew their strength," really change your life?

2. What promise of God have you been waiting to see fulfilled?

3. Are you fulfilling God's call on your life in thought, word, and deed?

4. Could you consider Saul's death by his own hand honorable or not?

5. How did David obey God and make the right choices that brought his community back together and out of danger in 1 Samuel?

6. "Return to your fortress, O prisoners of hope; even now I announce that I will restore twice as much to you" (Zech 9:12). Does this scripture speak to you? In what ways?

Guidepost VII

"He humbled himself and became obedient to death – even death on a cross!" (Phil 2:8)

Obedience

I feel quite confident, based on the word given below, that obedience really develops most fully in our discipleship walk after we have really learned all the previous lessons because it is so very difficult for us humans who have a rebellious nature due to the fall. I know I had to learn to sacrifice everything, to suffer yet glorify my God, and to carry on with perseverance, knowing that He would provide my every need (His promises are True), which experience and the word taught me is true! My life and faith walk was very long and torturous before I could humbly crawl up that mountain called *absolute obedience* to a Holy God. Now, humbly, I ask you to listen to the word of the Lord:

In obedience, walk the narrow road; ascend the craggy cliff wall; choose the difficult path, for I will then guide and place each of your steps upon my choice foothold, and no slip will occur, no ankle turned, no landslide will dislodge you from my path.

In obedience, a heart full of trust and faith grows to enormous proportions, and the fig tree will bear fruit at my command because it is always ready, in season and out.

In obedience, you will worship the Father alone and place no idols before Him! You will cease to erect idols that are meaningless to your purpose. It becomes easy for you to fortify that purpose with choices that Honor our Father alone. As He responds in trust to you and your indwelling capacity is filled with meaningful acts of service, your fruit will fill others and satiate your own hunger, a hunger for the Father's Love! Be obedient, child! Receive my blessing!! A filling of the heart to exceed every ability of human emotion to express.

You saw my Authority on Earth in My SON. My honor when desecrated (by Saul in his weakness, by David in lust and murder, by Hezekiah in pride and boasting, by the Jewish nation in rejecting My Son at the time of our visit); that Honor, which was decreed and set forth, was avenged. And it is absolute today! My Commandment is:

Serve Me alone!

Build no idols.

Love Me, love your neighbor.

Shema Israel, Adonai Elohenu, Adonai Echad! Hear o Israel, the Lord Our God, the Lord is One.

Jerusalem, Israel

Our last day in Israel began with a drive up onto the Mount of Olives, where one can drink in the magnificent view of the city of our God and imagine what Jesus saw each time He walked there. We then descended to the Garden of Gethsemane and entered into a private time of devotion, contemplation, prayer, and personal worship. This was deeply moving for all of us in personal ways. I wanted to plant a mustard seed but found that I had none. However, as I sat beneath a beautiful old olive tree, the Lord showed me a burnt seed on the ground that I could use as my "sacrificial burnt offering." I was reminded recently that this burnt offering meant so much to me because, in ancient times, the burnt offering was never a meal to be consumed. Rather, the ashes of the offering, totally consumed by fire on the altar, were removed outside the camp, mixed with water, and then used for the ritual purification. I felt its significance in the garden but had not made that connection immediately. God was purifying me, and I wasn't even aware of it. With this sacrificial symbol in hand, I prayed, interceding for all of Israel and the raising up of His messianic era priests, for our group, and for family and friends. I remembered Phil. 2:8, the painful moments our Lord spent in this very garden, and I rededicated myself to *"know Christ and the power of his resurrection and the fellowship of sharing in his sufferings, becoming like him in his death."* Phil 3:10 Then, taking two twigs, I wrapped them together in a cross secured with a strong reed, buried that seed and placed the cross over it. The magnitude of this symbolic act was again revealed in the day that followed.

Why Obedience

Not that I have already attained, or am already perfected; but I press on, that I may lay hold of that for which Christ Jesus has also laid hold of me. [13] Brethren, I do not count myself to have apprehended; but one thing I do, forgetting those things which are behind and reaching forward to those things which are ahead, [14] I press toward the goal for the prize of the upward call of God in Christ Jesus. Philippians 3:12-14

This scripture speaks so clearly to the pressing in and onward toward that for which Christ Jesus has called us into this incomparable, intimate, and passionate relationship with Him. You can hear that in Paul's voice, can't you? He had just stated that he wants to know Christ and the power of His resurrection and the fellowship of **sharing in His sufferings!** That's a bold, even brazen, statement, isn't it? Or is it? Whether or not he heard directly from His Savior's lips in a vision or dream or from those who were writing the history of the Gospels, Paul knew that His Lord had told His apostles that they would be persecuted and many would die painful deaths, like His. So how can one be obedient to such a Lord, even "obedient unto death"? Why do we press into this life of obedience, hunger, and thirst for the next word from our Lord, anxious to just do what He tells us to do? Where, in short, does this passion come from that called Christ forward to the cross and Paul to beatings, persecution, suffering, sickness, and imprisonment until death? A little bit of Bible history is necessary here to gain full understanding.

After the Garden of Eden

Alright, so we know that Eve and Adam blew it big time when the first temptation came along, and she, then he, were disobedient. Prior to the covenants God made, first with Abraham and then with Moses, God tried to restart His whole plan by causing the flood and allowing only Noah and his family to escape. After that event, He promised with the covenant of the rainbow never to curse the ground by flood again. The seed of sin quickly resurfaced in Noah, however, and God said of man that "every inclination of his heart is evil from his youth." ^{Gen 8:21} I must accept that, clearly, God had a plan and a purpose in allowing the fall of mankind. I don't think we ever understand it fully, but we do know that a creature with free will who worships and glorifies God freely pleases God. And this is the ultimate purpose of man.

Now, that said, we learn that the spiritual and the temporal blessings of God were contingent upon the obedience of the Israelites from the beginning:

> Now if you <u>obey</u> me fully and keep my covenant, then out of all nations you will be my treasured possession. Although the whole earth is mine, you will be for me a kingdom of priests and a holy nation. ^{Exodus 19:5}

No doubt that Moses, upon hearing this from the Lord on Mt. Sinai, was highly motivated to engage all the elders of the people and gain their trust, cooperation, and absolute commitment to such a high calling. The incredible story in Exodus relating the deliverance of the Ten Commandments is replete with examples of how Moses and the people and Aaron and the Priests were to obey God fully and cooperate with His intentions to birth a covenant for them that would be the foundation of God's holy nation.

In an excellent commentary by an unknown author, I read, "God provided Israel with "every facility for becoming the greatest nation on the earth." When they "brought forth wild grapes" instead of the mature fruit of character, He inquired, "What could have been done more to my vineyard, that I have not done in it?" ^{Isaiah 5:1-7} There was nothing God could have done for them that He did not do, yet they failed. It was "their unwillingness to submit to the restrictions and requirements of God" that "prevented them, to a great extent, from reaching the high standard which He desired them to attain, and from receiving the blessings which He was ready to bestow upon them."

Approximately 700 years after the law was given to Moses, by the time of Isaiah's rise as a prophet in 740 b.c. and Jeremiah's call to prophesy in 627 b.c., the Father was preparing His errant nation to receive something new in the way of a "covenant."

I, the Lord, have called You in righteousness, And will hold Your hand;
I will keep You and give You as a covenant to the people,
As a light to the Gentiles,
[7] To open blind eyes,
To bring out prisoners from the prison,
Those who sit in darkness from the prison house." Isaiah 42:6-7

"Behold, the days are coming, says the Lord, when I will make a new covenant with the house of Israel and with the house of Judah." Jer. 31:31

And Then Christ Came;

For this is My blood of the new covenant, which is shed for many for the remission of sins. Matt 26:28

He has made us competent as ministers of the new covenant, not of the letter but of the Spirit; for the letter kills, but the Spirit gives life. 2 Cor 3:6

And this is love, that you walk in obedience to his commandments!! 1 John 1:6

And the Glory of the New Covenant was revealed!

"But if the ministry of death (referring to the old covenant), written and engraved on stones, **was glorious**, so that the children of Israel could not look steadily at the face of Moses because of the glory of his countenance, which glory was passing away, [8]**how will the ministry of the Spirit not be more glorious?** 2 Cor 3:6-8

"For if that first covenant had been faultless, then no place would have been sought for a second. [8] Because finding fault with them, He says: "Behold, the days are coming, says the Lord, when I will make a new covenant with the house of Israel and with the house of Judah" Heb. 8:7-8

I wonder if, as a parent, perhaps you had this same experience: when your children are young, you are determined to raise them up "right"! You have all the best intentions; you provide them with the rules and instruct them in the "ways they should" go, offering encouragement and plenty of discipline along the way. You were told that they had to learn to respect you from the beginning and be obedient, so maybe you were a little bit too tough, demanding, or rigid with your rules. All for their own good, right?

And then, they grew into their own cognitive and personal awareness; liking their independence, they discovered that they could get away with doing things their way. Rebellion seeped in or took over! As they matured, whether or not they were obedient to you became less and less important, and sometimes you resorted to phrases like "just get them through it" and "pick your battles." (credit is due here to Dr. James Dobson).

How like God with the children of Abraham! And our children, like the Israelites in the desert following Moses in circles, and like those same Israelites who later demanded a king "just like all the other kids" when they grew weary of trying to decipher and obey a fearsome Heavenly Father! The Father had a plan since before the foundations of the earth to give us His one and only Son in a new covenant that would open the way for us to hunger and thirst for righteousness! We first receive the indwelling of the Holy Spirit, designed to mature and to grow us in Christ, when we believe in Jesus, and the love of the Father flows into our lives in amazing and powerful ways, making obedience to such love an absolute "NO BRAINER," as my kids would have said. In due time, the equipping ministry of the Holy Spirit empowers us and gives gifts or the fruit for the ministry of Christ that makes us effective.

Are we not, as parents, somewhat like God who, seeing that our children have become stubbornly entrenched in their rebellion, even prodigals, throw up our hands in resignation, cease our futile efforts to reign them in, and, instead, when they finally "come to their senses," offer them a new deal? One full of grace, mercy, and forgiveness? Then, in our undying love, we recommit to unconditional love for our children and prayerfully begin to wait for God to do what only He can do to change them. This waiting or patient endurance is essential. We do nothing because we must not get in God's way with our fleshly efforts.

To walk in obedience, something else is necessary.

We have seen that the fear of the Lord was a very good motivation for obedience during the early years of the old covenant Israelites. But insufficient in God's estimation, apparently. He added to it the salvation and forgiveness of sins through the New Covenant in Christ Jesus, and we continue to fail to obey. In fact, Jesus knew we would be incapable of obedience to His new standards. But God had a plan! He sent the Holy Spirit so that we could communicate intimately with Him, hear His voice, and obey His every nudge, making our thoughts, our emotions, and our lives one with the Lord's.

THE QUESTION: There continues to be a huge gap for most of us between the Lord's will, spoken in the Word, whispered in our souls, and shared through the gifts of knowledge, teaching, and prophecy, as well as the acts of mercy and service. What can possibly bridge that gap and bring us into harmony with the will of God? Is there some supernatural way to bring this ability to life, put it into action, flip the switch to "on," and know we are in His will always?

The answer is yes, but-- wait for it...

We must address the fact that there are major blockages that must be removed in every believer's life: the harassment of the enemy through oppression, our fallen, sinful nature that refuses to die quietly, our yearning for position, status, recognition of our abilities, and the love of others (and ourselves), and, of course, the pharisaical church in every age that encroaches on our freedoms in Christ.

My Testimony on Disobedience

As I began this final edit of the book and came to obedience, I was convicted that I needed to be transparent and really dig into how disobedience changed the course of my life and my faith.

Since I grew up in the culture of "If it feels good, do it" and was basically unchurched from my teen years on, I really did not take on the Christian change in lifestyle as quickly as others did. I saw myself as pretty free to act as I felt at the moment and did not attend church steadily. After about three years of seeking hard after Jesus, influences of the world crept in. I was regularly tempted by new attractive and fascinating men in my life, and then the social justice culture came along with community organizing ala Saul Alinsky with Marxist values and hard drinking included. Then, the feminist movement caused me to pause and re-evaluate my gender identity. Yes, as long ago as the mid-70s, this was introduced and entrapped many.

In my early 20s, I was so desperately wounded and depressed, rejected, and confused about my identity when I came to Christ that after a few years, I was seduced, for a time, into the powerful burgeoning feminist movement of the 70s. I was a radical feminist, establishing safe houses for battered women, as well as an agent for the War against Poverty. This involved working for the Community Action Commission as an advocate for the poor and a community organizer, trained in Chicago by the Saul Alinsky school of community organizers.

As a result, I was influenced to experiment with a bisexual lifestyle. Even though married, I did not consider God's ways and believed instead that this longing I had for love and attention from another woman was legitimate. Traipsing the streets of my friend's city, I indulged in the fantasy of becoming a lawyer and an assertive, valuable community member. This was my latent male identity asserting itself. It never went much further than that fantasy and a few delicious bagels from some unidentifiable bakery.

I eventually realized that it might have been the result of living with an alcoholic mother, who, deeply wounded in her own right, had little attention to give to me, especially since the time of my older sister's suicide, followed soon after by my father's death from cancer. I was 13 and 14 then. My mother had given her all to us when I was a child. She faithfully raised us five children in an "Ozzie and Harriet" type home, even though I knew we had some major cracks in our foundation as I grew up. I had received so much from her. But when our family came unglued, she had nothing more to say, to give, or to impart from her broken world. By the age of 24 or 25, I yearned for the companionship of women and began to believe that the feminist version of love might hold the key to happiness.

In fact, all it held was a lot of other lonely and hungry young women like me who would attach to one another and seek the sustenance they lacked in a dependent relationship that occasionally involved sex, and then move on just as broken and confused as before.

Having known Christ for a brief time, I was blessed to have His Holy Spirit calling me back to Him. He was interceding for me before the Father. So, when I began feeling my life was like a worm torn in three ways between my husband, my God, and my new feminist, gay friend, I began again to seek truth in earnest prayer. One evening soon after, I chose to go to a prayer meeting on the campus near my home. I'd never been there before. That evening, the leader called out, "Someone here is dealing with the spirit of homosexuality," and I simply raised my hand in acknowledgment. A brief prayer of deliverance was spoken, and freedom in Christ was mine! That burden and guilt dissipated into thin air like so much dust before the breath of God! One "poof" from Him and the enemy had to flee. I walked out of there freely yoked to Jesus, never to turn back upon that path. I chose His way, His truth, and He gave me His life. At that time, it meant the restoration of my injured marriage and another attempt to restore that sadly broken, unhealthy, soul-tied relationship.

Fortunately, a brief return to a campus prayer meeting had released me from any delusions and disobedience in that area. But I was lost for a while and began to question my faith, even returning to the trough of Buddhism and Universalist humanistic beliefs. Eventually, my husband became enticed to follow the path of mammon, increasing his income somehow, and we moved to California. There I was introduced to the "Lifestyles of the Rich and Famous," with trips to Hollywood and parties where snorting cocaine through a rolled $100 bill was commonplace. I was disgusted finally when I found that our host and benefactor physically abused his girlfriend, and I took a big step back! At that time, I learned that I was pregnant and very happy to begin life anew with a baby in my arms, the greatest joy and love of my life since I met Jesus. First, I tried a Unitarian Church, which I found to be vacuous and empty. But, not surprisingly, having a baby, raising a child, and my California lifestyle was totally incompatible anyway, and I soon found myself seeking a divorce, flying home to the Midwest, and landing in a powerhouse, spirit-filled, very solid Presbyterian church. As I had been raised in that denomination, I think I felt very safe right away. It was familiar and comforting, and the Holy Spirit was so alive and active that I quickly fell deep into the arms of my Savior. He cleaned up this temple and released me from those past few years, and I became hungry for His truth about everything.

Returning to the Lesson:

Remember, I said wait for it...?

I just described the blockades that we need to overcome: briefly, we call them *sin, Satan, self, the world*, and *the Church*. As I just described above, every one of those blockades took over my undisciplined and disobedient life for about 7-8 years. When I was desperate and ready to listen, eager for God to act in my life by the power of the Holy Spirit, the overcoming work of rebuilding a life could begin.

Let's look at each of the five above: First, Sin.

In the New Testament, the greatest of theologians, the Apostle Paul, discusses the problem of sin as our nature, the law, the victory, and yet the reality of being enslaved to sin. He has famously said, "I do not understand what I do. For what I want to do I do not do, but what I hate, I do!" Rom 7:15 If you are hungry for more, I refer you to Romans 6 and 7, and you will get his full discourse.

For my money, I like the book of James, written by our Lord's brother. Perhaps because he wasn't the Pharisee with years of training that Paul was, he states the problem more succinctly:

When tempted, no one should say, "God is tempting me." For God cannot be tempted by evil, nor does he tempt anyone; but each person is tempted when they are dragged away by their own evil desire and enticed. Then, after desire has conceived, it gives birth to sin; and sin, when it is full-grown, gives birth to death. James 1: 13-15

First, then, we must "own it." Don't blame Satan first, and definitely not God! Own it and humbly admit our failures to the Lord. Then He is able to lift us up. Only He can do this work, and only He can save us. So many of us have experienced deliverance prayers, inner healing of the residue of our fallen existence, and freedom in Christ from oppressive and obsessive irrational unhealthy thinking and behaviors. We know that he whom the Son sets free is free indeed!

Now the Lord is the Spirit, and where the Spirit of the Lord is, there is **freedom** 2 Cor 3:17

It is for **freedom** that Christ has set us free. Stand firm, then, and do not let yourselves be burdened again by a yoke of slavery. Galatians 5:1

Paul says this in **2 Corinthians 5:7-9 (NIV):**

[7] For we live by faith, not by sight. [8] We are confident, I say, and would prefer to be away from the body and at home with the Lord. [9] So we make it our goal to please him, whether we are at home in the body or away from it.

Live by faith to please Him!

You know that only God knows the thoughts and the intentions of our hearts. And He knows who has the desire to please Him and is seeking to be obedient.

Jesus said, "Do not let your hearts be troubled. **Trust in God**; Trust also in me.[Jn 14:1]

And later:

"Remain in me, and I will remain in you" [John 15:4]

Trust in God and our Lord. **Abide** in Him.

[13] But when he, the Spirit of truth, comes, he will guide you into all the truth. He will not speak on his own; he will speak only what he hears, and he will tell you what is yet to come. [John 16:13 (NIV)]

Listen to the Spirit of Truth.

But we ask, How do I know I am hearing the Spirit of Truth? Jesus says, *"He will bring glory to me. Taking from what is mine and making it known to you."* [John 16:14]

Glory will be brought to Jesus our Lord, and **none other.**

Second: Satan

Dear friends, do not believe every spirit, but test the spirits to see whether they are from God, because many false prophets have gone out into the world. This is how you can recognize the Spirit of God: Every spirit that acknowledges that Jesus Christ has come in the flesh is from God, but every spirit that does not acknowledge Jesus is not from God. This is the spirit of the antichrist, which you have heard is coming and even now is already in the world. 1 John 4:1-3

Test the spirits. If you are listening to God, writing or speaking His Word, receiving a message in a vision or dream, and you begin to doubt that you are hearing Him, do not be afraid to stop and ask, "Is this the Spirit of the Lord Jesus Christ speaking, my Savior who came in the flesh and died and rose again?" The Lord respects our testing and reassures us because He has commanded us not to be afraid. Don't be afraid to say, for example, "If this is any other spirit than the Spirit of Jesus Christ, my savior, in Jesus' name, I command you to be silent and to leave now." In my experience, you will feel clear and sure about your listening experience as God is not a God of chaos or fearful, inexplicable experiences.

Elsewhere in this book, we discuss the way in which we can pray so that demonic oppression does not rule our lives and separate us from God.

Third: Self

Elevating ourselves and seeking fame, recognition, or status is the antithesis of living the life that Jesus recognizes as befitting a child of God. There are almost too many scriptures to quote about humility. The entire gospel is paradoxical as He describes how the first will be last, how we should take the lowest station at the table, and how we must wash one another's feet. "Blessed are the meek for they will inherit the earth" and "Blessed are the poor in spirit (humble and hungry to learn) for theirs is the kingdom of heaven." Everything Jesus did was counter-cultural. So why is it so hard for us? It's our Pride. Pride is what the world cultivates in us and considers essential to a successful life. So simple, so huge and so very difficult to overcome. We must die to ourselves as written in Galatians 5:24: "Those who belong to Christ Jesus have crucified the flesh with its passions and desires."

Be Humble.

Fourth: The World

Here is the biggest stumbling block to those Christians who seem to have it together and are following hard after Jesus. We want to be assured of success even as Christians. How many of us can take off on a journey for weeks or months, carrying no supplies for the journey and intending to rest in God's provision as Jesus commanded His disciples? We learn early on not to "store up our treasures on earth" and to believe that we should not worry about life, what we eat, drink, or wear, because the Father knows that we need these things. Matt 6:25-32 "Do not worry about tomorrow, for tomorrow will worry about itself." Matt 6:34 But when does faith cause our beliefs to become active in this area? It is so much easier to measure success against the world's standards instead of God's. So we become either worldly-minded or, sadly, just quit trying.

Why is this so very difficult for us? I think it's because we have made it all about us—what God wants for us, how God wants to bless us, how we can be the most perfect Christians leading the most beautiful, awesome, abundant life and prove to the world that it's worth their while to follow Jesus. In short, it's the prosperity gospel in all its iterations over the centuries. Didn't the early Catholic church busy itself with accumulating riches and building glorious cathedrals as well as sometimes very comfortable quarters for a monastic lifestyle? And the church continues today to put its wealth on display to the world, and we benefit from the status attached to our buildings, our programs, and even our missions. That is crass and self-absorbed living, but there are many subtle ways faith becomes all about us, and we truly believe that if God isn't protecting us from every evil in this world, then "What's the point?"

> True religion that the Father accepts as pure and faultless is this: to look after orphans and widows in their distress and to keep oneself from being polluted by the world. James 1:27

Fifth: The "Pharisaical" Legalistic Church

The church has done much to spread the gospel and change the culture as a whole for the good. Yet when it negatively affects individuals through legalistic training, it damages and suffocates the spirit that is longing after God. This is the condition that prohibits many from leaning into and trusting that a loving God can be followed obediently and that the freedom of the abundant life in the Spirit can truly begin. This problem is widespread, and I know many who have sought counseling for relief from the thorns of toxic religious upbringing. For most, it began in childhood with strict rules and frequent shaming of those who fail to measure up. Often, abuse and purposeful deprivation were involved. As a consequence, it is so deeply ingrained that often, it will take many years of re-education and prayerful inner healing to undo the damage.

God is Good and Nurtures Life; He is Not Toxic!

As I described in my own life, when the blockades have been dealt with, then we can move into that place of growth and restoration! And for some, it is all at once and glorious freedom. But even if the hurdles are taken slowly over the years, it's fine! Don't compare yourself to others because God is doing this sanctifying work in each of us in His timing.

> And whatever you do, whether in word or deed, do it all in the name of the Lord Jesus, giving thanks to God the Father through him. Col 3:17

Whatever you do, work at it with all your heart, as working for the Lord, not for human masters, Col 3:23

JUST DO IT! Act in accordance with what direction you have received through all the ways we can walk in intimate communion with our Lord

To summarize the final step, I believe in obedience, after all purposeful and deliberate actions are done, we must:

- Have faith
- Desire to please God
- Trust God
- Abide in Him
- Listen to Him speak
- Know He will glorify Jesus
- Test the spirits
- Be humble
- Know He is good, not toxic
- Act in obedience

Obedience: A Testimony to His Faithfulness

In the last few years, the Lord has tested me and led me on the path of obedience in ministry on a new and higher level of trust. Knowing that my heart's desire was to be in ministry full-time, I listened and waited patiently for Him to release me from work at the Christian counseling center where I had been for five years. I loved my work and the way in which He had led me to incorporate freedom and healing prayers with Rational Christian Emotive therapy. I was so blessed to witness many clients grow in the Lord and walk into their identity in Christ that I knew that I was there to do the Lord's work as long as He desired. Then, one day, I heard His still, small voice whisper, "I am taking you out of the marketplace and into my provision." He bolstered this announcement with the scripture I love from Romans 8:28, "God works all things together for good for those who love Him and are called according to His purpose." Hearing these words from my Lord was followed the next Sunday by hearing the exact same words from my friend as he gave his testimony at church about God's call to ministry: "I am taking you out of the marketplace and into my provision." Not only that, but when the fishbowl full of scriptures was passed around, I pulled out ... ROMANS 8:28! We often like to say that there are no coincidences in God's ways. I walked out of that position as a licensed professional clinical counselor and into that of a shepherdess who guides others into healing prayer and spiritual growth. But the obedience didn't stop there.

Now that our income was cut a bit and my husband longed to retire from his 40+ years of labor, the Lord began a work in me to remove the "perception of the world" from my view. This began with a time of deep repentance in the 40 days leading up to the Day of Atonement on the Jewish calendar. I had to repent of all my worldly, jealous, covetous attachments to my family's vacation cottage in Wisconsin. This was a place that was more like home to me than any house I have ever lived in, and it held the best and longest-lasting memories of my long-ago "Ozzie and Harriet" time growing up. Although it was no longer technically mine by ownership, I had a deep emotional investment in it and a longing to own, control, improve, and use it more and more. God had to pry it out of my hands, spiritually speaking, and show me how it was merely a substitute for what I really longed for: to know the depth of my worth in Him! Oh, how He rewards those who walk in obedience with Him! After relinquishing my petty, selfish desires, He began to fill me with the deepest wisdom and knowledge of and feeling of my worth in Christ that I have ever known. I will share that word in a moment. Oh, and a year later, I received the deed, which made me the owner of a very small percentage of that place. God is a mystery!

The next thing God did for me and my husband was to release us from the home we loved but could not afford to stay in and retire. The Lord helped us sell it in a day without a realtor the same week that we made an offer on our new home: a log cabin home in the country! He managed our finances to give us the new home completely paid for with proceeds from the previous one! He is such a good, good Father! He is the one who fulfills all His promises, provides all our needs, and knows the deepest desires of our hearts. "For I know the plans I have for you, plans to prosper you and not to harm you, plans to give you *My* hope and *My* future!" [Jer. 29:11] (italicized words added) He wants us to call on Him, to come and pray to Him. He says He will listen. We will find Him because He says, "I will be found by you!" [Jer. 29:14]

Be obedient, seek Him, and be found by God. Hear His still, strong voice:

Fast on my word. Devour, know deeply and live on my word.

Consume Me daily, and I am incorporated into the substance of who you are. What you think and say. Make no room within for the lies of the enemy—I am a Jealous God, protector of my Temple! I see the innermost holy of places that shines with glistening white quartz in you. No darkness shadows or clings to the facets of purity in your inner being, my temple!

But my light bounces and reflects from each crystal to the next and the next! The most glorious of inner sanctums are you when the darkness of the enemy has been vanquished. This is purity! This is my throne room; when you enter the Holy of Holies, I enter you!

Our Key for this Journey: Remember that you are His Temple, and He wants to have free access to that Temple!

Reflections

1. What is the area of your life that you find most difficult to bring into submission and obedience?
2. Have you repented of it repeatedly and still find its persistent presence is hanging on?
3. Do you resent God's required obedience in our lives, even unto death? This, too, requires repentance.

Ask God to show you the key to unlock these areas of resistance. He has promised that He would provide everything we need! And read on to the next chapter and be further equipped!

4. What are the most beautiful gifts you have received when you experienced radical obedience?
5. How has obedience changed your life?

Guidepost VIII

Release the Blessing

I have often wondered how these guideposts just seemed to "write themselves." Even now, I am in awe of how Father's words to me as I listened to Him in Israel describe the process or the steps of the pathway I had taken, would be taking, and was to share with others. This was His demonstration of how we "Release the Blessing." I know that many Christians mature much earlier than I did, and that's ok. We come from so many varied backgrounds! Because I took that long detour to Woodstock and Transcendental Meditation rather than entering a Christian seminary, for example, I was a late bloomer, and my consciousness of discipleship steps had to be worked out slowly, one guidepost at a time. Others, maybe those who read these words, may rush to "Release their Blessings" to others. I caution only that they check their hearts and spirits for faith in Christ and maturity to the point of unquestioning obedience before leaping into the fires of ministry.

I begin with a beautiful word from our Father of Lights:

Thank you, beautiful remnant children! For hearing me, for seeking me, for willingly releasing your hearts of burden for my yoke of love, thank you for trusting me and in faith opening the river of grace to freely run in your lives. My longing for you is being fulfilled in your intimate love language, the same as mine, heard by ears and eyes unveiled! Thank you for coming to me on your knees! I bless the nail-scarred hands through which I see you for boldly proclaiming My word of Truth; I seek the deaf who may hear your voices, for they are beautiful voices. My time of Harvest will open the closed and veiled faces to receive the glory of My splendor, and the deaf will hear what you have heard!

(Even now, the weight of His love in this message is so great I can barely type it!) I paused and eventually asked, 1) What about the condemned? and 2) How should I enter in now to the throne room?)

Father says, "You need not wonder, for my throne room is among you each time you gather." Then, slowly take my shearing pen among the sheep and remove their wool. The wolves will howl with greed, but my Shepherd's crook will not fail to gather the naked and afraid to me. Be not afraid, as <u>We Are ONE</u>. The shorn wool will be as a home for the broken and a place for the weary. This wool is the buffer of the world that clings to us until it is shorn away!

As I read these beautiful God-inspired words once again, I am struck by the power and the unique tone and images He uses to inspire us. We are being thanked by our Lord for joining with Him in His amazing work of redemption, for hearing and seeking Him and taking upon ourselves His yoke in order to do the good works He has created in and for us to do before the foundations of the earth. He sees us as fully His partners in releasing the blessings of what we have received and what we have heard into the Harvest fields! He equips us with the shearing pen and the Shepherd's crook. It is a work of the Father's heart upon which we, His remnant children, embark as we go up to Jerusalem.

My Story Revisited: The Blessing Released

Another important chapter in my life has been the healing of a deeply wounded little girl's heart and the long-ago death of her father. My heavenly Father was such a distant and intangible figure to me for most of my Christian walk. Like so many others, the father image was spoiled in childhood. This is why:

Although we started off well, and I have fond memories at an early age of eating too much pie at our favorite local restaurant, laughing and smiling at my dad, pretty soon I grew into a strong-willed little girl. At the age of 6 or 7, I remember my dad telling me to leave the room where he was resting, and I responded in a very sassy voice, saying, "Yes, your royal highness." I ran up the stairs, he followed, and I got a well-deserved "whooping" with the belt! Ouch! Right or wrong, I was in pain, very angry, and began to develop a deep hatred toward Dad then and there. I was very, very good at holding onto that bitterness and resentment. So good, in fact, that I never again had a close relationship with him. Yes, he did try to mend the fences, but words of comfort and love, or being held and comforted, were not in his vocabulary. He was German, stern, and mostly authoritarian.

And so it remained until the day that he died an early death, at the age of 53, when I was just 13. My mother encouraged me to read the 23rd Psalm to him at his bedside before he went to the hospital, and I am grateful now that I did. I was angry and very confused, but at least,

I believe, those were the last words I ever spoke to my father. I am glad they were the words of God.

Deep heart wounds are difficult and resistant to healing, and mine was no different. I forgave him multiple times. I even undid the belief system that had me trying to, somehow, subconsciously compete with "the boys" for my father's attention and the belief that if you are a woman, you are somehow second class. Onions have layers, as Shrek is so fond of saying. This healing was many years in the making.

Finally, last winter, one quiet grey day, I found myself sobbing in grief from a deep place for my father, Dr. John, whom everyone else loved and whom I had never really known. Not because of his early death but because in my rebellious state as a child, I never repented, asked for or received forgiveness, or gave him another chance to love me, if he could. I asked the Lord, "Why now, after all these years?" and He showed me that it was because I longed to know the meekness, humility, and purity of His heart that comes in forgiveness. And "in grief and longing for what never was allowed to grow," His still voice whispered, "You see your own stubborn, prideful heart as a child. And now, confess and repent; just as I long to be your Father, your father on Earth did as well, but he could not reach through the defense you erected against him." And oh, how I repented! I took that little child that I was to the cross of Jesus then and there and made that holiest of transactions anew at the foot of the cross for her and with her. We were made NEW! Washed and cleansed with the blood of the Lamb and the hyssop that makes us cleaner than snow.

That day, the Lord gave me the 51st Psalm for my life! I heard in my spirit that *"it is the deepest truth of my healing-life-giving sustenance. I flow in forgiveness into your deepest parts and give you My wisdom in the inmost place. Truth and wisdom must be your DNA. They rebuild the walls that have become permeable; they change the nucleus and remove the enemies' auto-destruct imprint. Repentance, forgiveness, and a pure heart must surround every broken and crushed 'bone,' and restoration begins within that place."*

And now this child, who has grown up into maturity in Christ and lives within me, wants only to give it all away and release the blessing of this deep inner healing. The wisdom imparted to me in this experience is not for me alone. It's for those who are open to the full truth of the power of God to transform their lives, no matter how old and forgotten or never recognized, their own wounds and sinful behavior. All of it is open for inspection; all of the layers can and will be peeled back; all of it healed by Abba Daddy. If healing your father's wound is part of your journey, you will finally arrive at the place where you are invited into your Father's inner sanctum, His Holy Throne Room, and never ever silenced, shushed, or chased out again.

Preparing to Release the Latter-Day Blessings

I want to now use as an example my testimony of how God led me to deal with the feelings described below as He prepared me to move on in my life from the attachment to my childhood happy place. I will go through my inner healing prayer model step by step below. First, there is, for me, some important context around when this healing occurred:

As I write this, we are in the month of Elul in the Jewish calendar. This begins the 40-day period of the year referred to as Yemei Ratzon—Days of Favor. It was during this time that the Lord forgave the people of Israel following the sin of the Golden Calf. According to Rishi, an 11th century rabbi, Moses ascended the mountain for the third time on Elul 1 for 40 days to invoke God's mercy and to complete atonement for the sins of the people. Here, he received the second set of tablets and descended the mountain on Tishri 10 or Yom Kippur.

So this is a time when we can also follow tradition, repent, and confess our sins up to the 40th day, which falls on Yom Kippur. It is considered especially prophetic to both Jews and Christians that this period began this year on the day that the complete solar eclipse crossed the United States from coast to coast. A complete solar eclipse is a significant sign that has traditionally been a signal to the people of the land to repent. This was true even when Jonah was sent to Nineveh to call them to repentance. Astrologists know that a total solar eclipse happened at the same time. Because they had suffered plague and famine and seen a total eclipse, they were willing to listen to Jonah and really hear his words of warning. They did repent and were saved (Jonah 3:10). Now, we in the United States must face this same beckoning from the Father. He desperately wants us to seek Him now.

Hear the word of the Lord impressed upon this listener the day of the solar eclipse seen in the Obed Wild Scenic River area of Tennessee, high on an overlook along the Cumberland Trail, above the confluence of the Emory and the Obed rivers:

This is the first day of your 40 days in the wilderness. You must fast and repent like never before. And pray, interceding for Me. I prepare you for the persecution. Forty days of wilderness removes the world from your perception. Eyes cannot see this Glory now. But listen to the background reverberations of overwhelmed systems and failing infrastructures. Extremely inflated worldly expectations crash in anger to the ground, and doors fly open. They (powers and authorities of this world) embark to hunt and devour my unprotected, unclothed body parts.

Be as Brides entered in, radiant in your countenance, lovely in my redeemed face; your armor is sharp and polished in the sands of time like a tumbled, polished gem!

Blunt your tongue. Sharpen your mind. Always be prepared to prophesy the testimony of Jesus with and in My Holy Spirit of Love.

I am now 10 days into this fasting and repentance, and I have never before experienced such a deep and intense period of purification. Father is leaving no stone unturned. Every bit of pride, greed, jealousy, covetousness, and lack of love for Father, myself, and others is being relentlessly illuminated within me as Abba shines His light in the darkness and shatters the dark in His grace and forgiveness!

> "Even the darkness will not be dark to you; The night will shine like the day. For darkness is as light to you" Ps 139:12

He is loving me and many of His remnant church into a place of readiness, I believe, so that when those who seek His Face in these later days rise up out of the ashes around them and come into places of truth and ministry for help, they will receive the blessings of His love perfected and be made whole!

The Path of Healing: The Model

This is the pattern Father has shown me in my own search in these "Days of Favor" as well as those with whom I have worked:

- **Confession.** This usually begins with a semi-reasoned attempt to explain to the Lord what has gone wrong in my life, my emotions, and my mind that seems to be in violation of His Perfect Peace. I seldom have the complete picture or understand it fully; I am frustrated with my thoughts and/or behavior and cannot change them! Like Paul says so well, "When I want to do good, evil is right there with me....waging war against the law of my mind and making me a prisoner of the law of sin at work within my members!... Who will rescue me from this body of death?" Rom. 7: 21-24

Testimony: Here is a true-life example...

Let me be very real here. I got to this lovely family place for my vacation, a whole week with just me, the dog, and the Lord! And I was a wreck. All I could think of was what was wrong with this cottage. What needed to be fixed, what new things we desperately needed, and how the exterior totally failed in its northern woods esthetic! I was consumed with envy, greed, covetousness, and jealousy. Where was my place of peace and joy? I cried out to Abba, and I confessed that it was painful. I hated seeing the ugly depths of my discontent and my sin.

- **Repentance:** At this point, we must move forward and, having felt the depth of our depravity, eagerly enter into the place of grace. Just a simple and sincere "Father, forgive ME!" is all our Father asks from us as we recommit our lives to complete obedience. And if we listen closely to Him, we may hear that loving "I forgive you" before we even utter the words.
- **Renounce the Spirits:** I know from experience that when my thoughts or emotions are out of control, spiritual warfare has set in. It is my practice to say

out loud, very firmly:

"Spirit of (fear, greed, lust, jealousy, etc.), in Jesus' name I renounce you. I cut you off; every binding and tie with you is severed! I cancel my agreement with you, I remove your authority over me, and I command you to go now, in Jesus' name! And I now shut the door on you and seal it shut by the power of the Name that is above every Name, the Name of Jesus."

This has become "normal Christian living," as my mentors taught me. Because we know that we have been given the authority to rebuke or renounce the spirits; just as Jesus gave it to His disciples, He has given it to us by the presence and the Power of the Holy Spirit in us. We can see this change within us and those we pray for almost instantly many times.

Example continued:

I want to say that it isn't hard to do this and also that it's not necessarily instantaneous or permanent either! This instance described above was a difficult battle, taking my attention for a day as I experienced the world around me with newly enlightened eyes. And it will be ongoing. This is because I am battling a lifelong pattern of substituting the things of this world for the precious Love of the Father. Every thought about things in this world that are not real needs or even genuine dreams and desires (which the Father does allow us) must be screened, and any hint of the old jealousy and covetousness will have to die and perhaps will require a rebuke if it is tenacious. Because, in my testimony above, the cottage is symbolic of my earthly father's love and care for us as a family, it got very complicated. But that tenacity is the clue to me that I'm dealing with the powers and authorities in this world and not simply my own thoughts.

- **Dig Out the Roots**: Usually, just following the rebuke of the spirit, when I am "soul searching," I will prayerfully ask Father:

"How did I ever get to this point, Lord? Where did this stuff come from? What kind of foothold did I open up to the oppressive spirit?"

He is faithful in showing me the connections to my life, the distant and the current, the traumas and the griefs, the losses and hurts that opened wounds in my soul. When we have been given that information, we can follow with more action to heal those hurtful places—either more deliverance prayer, perhaps a time of standing in the gap with another healing partner to release old pains, and sometimes the Lord just provides us the mental image of a new, whole, bright, and clean heart that He has created in us. These are just examples of how He heals. His creativity is endless and always specific to the needs of His children.

Example continues:

I really was astonished by how quickly the Lord answered my prayer this time to dig up the roots of my sin. Through a word of knowledge, He let me know that the early years of my life, which were lacking in love, had created in me a deep feeling of rejection and the belief that what I am would never be completely acceptable or good enough. Although I thought I had been healed of those pains, it was not complete. I still lacked love for myself. I learned that this condition, being separated from myself, was an opening for all the sin to enter. Just as in my earlier years when sex, drugs, and rock n roll were the drugs of choice, I continued to medicate the pain of this insufficiency with the stuff of this world, especially that cottage in Wisconsin.

- **Release the Blessing**: After the healing and the freedom from oppression, we release the blessings of scripture over those for whom we have prayed to speak truth into those places where darkness had dwelled, to encourage and direct them in their walk.

Example continues:

The Lord is quick to heal and spoke into my spirit very firmly from Ps 139: 13-14:

> "For you created me in my inmost being, You knit me together in my mother's womb. I praise you because I am fearfully and wonderfully made; Your works are wonderful, I know THAT full well."

When the Father of Lights gives you a scripture and tells you it is for you personally, you tend to listen and take it fully into your spirit, where He can then draw you up into the fullness of all you were created to be! I am well on the way now in the healing path He has laid before me. I have entered the shearing pen, and the buffer, the wool, of the world is being shorn away! Hallelujah and Praise God!

A dear friend recently taught a class at the Deeper Living Center about the effects of the world on Christians and how it can separate us from our walk and from the fellowship we deeply desire with the Lord and block us from the true depths of freedom we seek in Christ. Just as our sin, Satan, and self can separate us from fellowship, so can the world. This has been my experience: the world is a very fertile ground for pride, my sin, and oppressive spirits to settle in and take root. It is God's call to us all to teach on this subject today and alert the remnant to the stupor of the world, that buffer, like sheep's wool, in our culture today.

The Blessings of the Church through the Ages

I began to contemplate the enormity of the above subject, "The Blessings of the Church through the Ages," and how the world and the present culture evolved through the centuries to its present "post-Christian" state. I was frankly overwhelmed and daunted by a seemingly impossible task, a task about which volumes and volumes have already been written. Yet, I knew that Father had a message for us today that would put it succinctly into perspective from His viewpoint. So I asked the question: What is important for us today about the blessings of the church that have been poured out over centuries, Lord, changing the world from a barbaric, idolatrous place where human sacrifice was commonplace to a place where even the non-Christian mind believes in the ideals of world peace, opportunity, freedom, respect and equality for all? Here are the impressions and the understanding I received:

My church followed Me in Love, but some followed the rulers, powers, and authorities of this world into the lust for power. Growing up through the centuries side by side were great outpourings of love and compassion for the poor, my forgiveness of sin, and the impetus to eliminate human slavery and provide the means of sustenance to all. Simultaneously, the evil one attacked and devoured as many followers of the Way to whom he had gained access and corrupted love with an insatiable appetite for power and personal dominion. The wheat of my bread of life given to heal the world has grown up with the tares, the weeds, of destruction in its midst. It has always been so and must always be until the end of the age.

One by one, my children bring love and blessings

to enlighten the chosen and shatter their darkness, setting the captives free! Then I will come when all these signs have appeared and the wheat is thick for harvest.

From a historical viewpoint of the "growth of the church," this can make no sense to you because My ways are higher than yours. But the prophet Isaiah is true; he knew Me, and his word that the Gentiles would be brought in under My banner (Isa 49:22) is increasing daily into the fruition, the fullness of the kingdom of the Father, under My feet. I am the wisdom of all creation, the craftsman with the Father (Pro. 8:30) here before the foundations of the earth were laid. (Pro 8:23)

I Am the Lion of Judah about to roar like never before! Continue the thirst for righteousness, and I will fill your cups to overflowing with my gracious love and the healing power of forgiveness. You will walk in this way and rejoice with me before the throne of the Almighty Father of us all.

My prayer in writing this is that if the Lord speaks this truth to you, it will resonate and uplift you in your daily walk upon those paths that He raises up before you, because this is His promise:

"To say to the captives, 'Come out,' and to those in darkness, 'Be free!'
They will feed beside the roads and find pasture on every barren hill.
They will neither hunger nor thirst, nor will the desert heat or the sun beat upon them.
He who has compassion on them will guide them and lead them beside springs of water. <u>I will turn all my mountains into roads, and my highways will be raised up.</u> Isa. 9-10

Let the truth of the word of God always be your guide and your guidepost!

Reflections

1. Have you ever felt you experienced what the psalmist was talking about in this scripture: "Even the darkness will not be dark to you" (Psalm 139)? What was that like? What does that mean?
2. Have you prayed for someone in Jesus' name and did not feel the earth move? How can you reconcile that?
3. Does the Lord mean that when you walk with Him in His power to release His blessings that you will spiritually be "walking on water" every time?
4. What does "normal Christian living" consist of when we know that the demonic realm must retreat, scatter, disband, and cease their attack when we speak commands in the name of Yeshua?
5. How is it possible that speaking scripture over someone, just repeating words written in a scroll thousands of years ago, can release blessings and healing into another's life?
6. Do you know the scriptures that engage you with the authority of Christ to speak His word in His Name?

(I have not given them to you. This is a challenge for you to seek out the 'mystery' truth, for it is golden!)

Guidepost IX

Persecution

In my flesh, I resist with a deep, ancient fear, while holding onto worldly hope, the thought that persecution must be a Guidepost we encounter along the paths of righteousness as we walk on our way "Up to Jerusalem." I think we all resist this thought, which now seems to have become a solid reality. Jesus himself warned His disciples once they were prepared to go out into the world two by two to "Beware of men for they will hand you over to the courts and scourge you in the synagogues." Matt 10:17 This warning came rather late in His discipleship of the twelve, long after they had begun to walk with Him and their hunger for righteousness was producing the sanctification that Jesus knew would come. So, too, for us in these guideposts.

In January of 2017, this word was revealed to me:

Critical points intersect; My armies here will move, and lasting change convulses the earth. Horror and fear, but Terror <u>Not</u> to my people. Perched on hills above the plains and safety of eagles, breech the battle lines drawn in dust. No power on Earth nor physical manifestation of evil can overwhelm these *forces. Because My Hand is mightier, My heart is heavier; its weight will burst forth and drown the evil with Its love. Love is WORD, Love is LOGOS, it is POWER the evil one has not yet seen! ...Fear not, my little ones—the least of these; move into the shelter of My wings.*

On November 5, 2017, as those in my home fellowship were deep in study and prayer in remembrance of the persecuted church around the globe, Devin Patrick Kelley walked into a Baptist Church in Sutherland, Texas, and murdered 26 members of that congregation, wounded 20 and died himself by suicide. Was this persecution of the church?

"Devin Patrick Kelley, the 26-year-old who stormed First Baptist Church in Texas and shot and killed 26 and wounded scores more, was described by former school classmates as an "outcast" and atheist who used social media to mock Christianity."

(Quote taken from Cheryl K. Chumley, The Washington Times, November 6, 2017)

We will not likely receive much more news or deep analysis of this man's personality in total in the future since the media quickly and quite adamantly reported their belief that this act of violence was a result of the lack of gun control and a lethal weapon in the hands of a mentally unbalanced man with violent criminal behavior and domestic abuse in his past. Clearly, to the world, it is a case of a man with a personal vendetta against his former in-laws who attended that church and not a measure of the growing persecution of the Christian church. Yet, the in-laws were not even present on the day of the massacre. And over and over, Devin Kelley's former friends stated that he hated Christians and even "preached" his atheistic viewpoint on social media.

Will this happen again and with greater frequency? Our chances of being caught today in one of the 2 to 3 church shootings a year are minimal, according to Joe Carter, Editor of the *Gospel Coalition*:

> "There are an estimated 378,000 congregations in the United States, which means the likelihood of any congregation being involved in a shooting in any year is approximately one in 126,000 or 0.0000079 percent. That means your odds of being in a church service in which a shooting occurs are at most 1 in 6,552,000 or 0.00000015 percent." (November 6, 2017, thegospelcoalition.org)

However, the impact on the church as a whole body is acute pain, mourning, shock, and fear. Confusion may take over in some of us, which is exactly what the enemy, Satan, wishes to accomplish. Will we go underground and flee from our churches? Listen to this Word, also given on November 6, 2017:

If you must go underground to survive, you will! And the enemies will believe they are winning. Yet the fervor of my Body will grow steadily and erupt in joy just as the enemy sits back to rejoice in victory. Be wise as serpents yet gentle as doves. My church will attempt to police itself. Gunmen will assault the body again until the public church becomes sanitized and neutralized.

My love for you will never fail. Remember that I taught you that when you are brought before the rulers and authorities both in this world and in the church, My Spirit will teach you what to say, or you will say nothing. They have judged your beliefs as indefensible already so that there is little left to defend in the world. But you will glorify your Father who is in Heaven, *and you will do this from His throneroom. Release <u>all</u> that chains you to this world so that I may move you as I will, and you will transcend the times and the places that have preceded you. You will understand what this means when you have broken free.*

I also resist writing about persecution because, after all, what do I know about persecution from my perspective as a sheltered, mid-western, pampered Christ-follower? Yet the Father insists:

Do not believe that the remnant can escape the persecution that followed My Son in His journey up to Jerusalem. It is inevitable that with the release of your blessing, the enemy will strike. And yet, if in the revelation of my Truth that instills courage and obedience and there is oneness with my joy and healing presence, how can His suffering and persecution not exist?

We co-exist with Christ. *"I no longer live, but Christ lives in me."* Gal 2:19 He has freed me from my chains for His purposes into His joy and abundant life, to release His blessings, healings, and freedom. There is no question but that in our mix of suffering will come persecution. It is the enemy's last desperate attempt to suppress the Truth in each of us! Yet, Jesus told us plainly to expect and to accept it, emphasizing that it is a blessing! Matt 5: 10-12 Our natural flesh recoils, but the Spirit-man rejoices because it understands what the natural man cannot! Our Spirit-man says:

"I want to know Christ and the power of his resurrection and the <u>fellowship of sharing in his sufferings, becoming like him in his death,</u> and so, somehow to attain to the resurrection from the dead." Phil 3: 10-11

The Subtle Persecution

Today's believers in the United States often suffer a subtler form of persecution. It sounds like denigration of our choices in lifestyle, being mocked for our biblical morals, or insulted because we choose not to engage in some activities when they interfere with our obligations to church, family, and God. Psalm 109 describes what it has felt like to this believer when family members or those formerly in fellowship with me have turned against me:

[1]God, whom I praise,
do not be silent,
[2] for the mouths of wicked and deceitful people
are opened against me;
they speak against me with lying tongues.
[3] They surround me with hate-filled words,
attacking me for no reason.
[4] Instead of receiving my love, they accuse me,
though I continue in prayer.
[5] They devise evil against me instead of good,
and hatred in place of my love.

We have found that a powerful divisive spirit has arisen in the church and sometimes creates havoc among believers. The attacks that come when this spirit is active feel like "no reason." This has occurred because of splits along political party lines, for example, causing disrespect for authority in our local community as well as national governmental authority. It is essential that we recognize that a foothold for the critical spirit has been created in each of us, and the enemy has taken up his position in the church with his usual motive to devour and destroy the body of Christ. In addition, we have seen the usual theological splits grow deeper and wider between those of different faith movements as many anxiously await revival, an outpouring of extreme signs and wonders, and the second coming. With some, there is such a hunger to experience God in powerful ways that even ancient occult methods, divination, fortune telling, eastern meditation, and the worship of angels, clearly forbidden in scripture, are seeping back into some churches. To say "no, thank you" to these methods is viewed as unreasonable, narrow-minded, or rigid legalistic faith to some.

Then there are those who are being openly challenged in the courts because they made statements about their faith at work, school, or sporting events, or they prayed in public (even at the bedside of a sick and dying individual) or refused to support immoral lifestyles with one's personal business. We, "Followers of the Way," stand at the precipice, and all wonder when we will be accused of "stepping over the line" and taken before the Sanhedrin of today's society.

A Step Back into Jesus's Time

You are blessed if you have entered into the new covenant, received the Holy Spirit, and are now able to understand these things revealed to you in the Mind of Christ, who receives everything from the Father.

Imagine if you were a Galilean of Jesus' day sitting on the mountain and hearing these words:

"Blessed are those who have been persecuted for the sake of righteousness, for theirs is the kingdom of heaven.

"Blessed are you when people insult you and persecute you and falsely say all kinds of evil against you because of Me. Rejoice and be glad, for your reward in heaven is great; for in the same way they persecuted the prophets who were before you."

If you were that simple Galilean, uneducated, a close

disciple of the Lord's, or a farmer, a fisherman, a crafts-man, or a tradesman, lost in a life of sin, do you think that you would have said,

"YES! Unequivocally, YES, that's the man I want to follow and serve and somehow become just like him!"

I don't think I could have begun to comprehend what Jesus was proposing to me, unless...

Unless my ancestral heritage was steeped in the memory of persecution: 400 years of enslavement, followed by redemption, freedom, and prosperity! Followed again by persecution, captivity, and enslavement for 70 years! And again, freedom, redemption, and rebuilding the temple and Jerusalem. Followed by more persecution and the restoration in the time of the Maccabees. Either way, I would be intrigued by this man who had already gone throughout Galilee, preaching and teaching and healing every disease and sickness, whose fame had spread all over Syria, and who healed all who were brought to Him. Why were these large crowds following Him from Galilee, the Decapolis, Jerusalem, Judea, and the region across the Jordan?

My Belief

I think the answer was as simple for them as it was for me. I began to love and serve Jesus when I accepted the truth *that He gave His life for me*, forgave all my sins, and sent His Holy Spirit to comfort and guide me. Those early followers had not yet received that incomparable gift of the Holy Spirit, but they did see Him give of Himself, selflessly and without reserve, performing miracles of healing and later feeding huge crowds. "What if He is our long-awaited Messiah?" they asked one another, trying to comprehend what kind of man He was. He earned their respectful attention! Sadly, many, even most, would not continue to follow Him to His untimely, God-ordained end through persecution but eventually turned away.

Testimonies: My Slower Path from Loving Him to Dying if Need Be

Without the face-to-face experience of the disciples, I grew more slowly in the love of the Lord and the presence of His Spirit over the years. Truthfully, I grew closer to that willingness to die for His incomparable love when the reality of His healing touch began to set me free from all my bondages, Including all the demons that initially possessed me (prior to accepting Him into my life), then from those that oppressed me, occupying my thoughts and emotions for many years as a Christian.

As Christians, We Do Not Persecute Others, nor do we judge those outside the Church! I recognize that one of the most vehement voices of persecution against the church in the USA today are those of the LGBTQ community. In their fear of perceived prejudice from the Church, they lash out to establish the right to their existence. They cannot begin to understand the depth of love and freedom they have been truly given, to choose how they live in this world from those of us who are part of the remnant church of Jesus Christ, we who "judge no one from a worldly point of view." [2 Cor 5:16-19] We know that we have not been sent to judge the world and most of us have lived and sinned a good while in the world! We know what we have been given in Christ and would never judge those who do not choose to come to Christ. This is my testimony to that truth.

In the chapter on Obedience, I touched on a time in my life as a Christian in my early 20s when I lived more in the world than in the love of God. However, the Lord sought me out and changed me! Allow me to repeat a short piece of the end of that testimony here to make my point.

When I was confused and feeling torn apart:

I began again to seek truth in earnest prayer. One evening soon after, I chose to go to a prayer meeting on the campus near my home. I'd never been there before. That evening, the leader called out, "Someone here is dealing with the spirit of homosexuality," and I simply raised my hand in acknowledgment. A brief prayer of deliverance was spoken, and freedom in Christ was mine! That burden and guilt dissipated into thin air like so much dust before the breath of God! One "poof" from Him and the enemy had to flee. I walked out of there freely yoked to Jesus, never to turn back upon that path. I chose His way, His truth, and He gave me His life.

My experience has given me a "God's Eye Perspective" on the choice I made to walk away from the Lord, His desire to call me back to Him and free me from a spiritual attack, and lastly, to give me the clear knowledge that it was He alone and not being judged by the church for my sin, that allowed me to grasp His hand and follow. How, then, could I ever dare judge another person for the same?

My Testimony: A Time of Persecution Through Witchcraft

Now that I am old, and God has revealed so much more truth and wisdom to me, I have been able to put together some very uncomfortable and disturbing facts that reveal the power and the danger that the enemy has amassed in today's world steeped in Satanism and witchcraft. This persecution by the enemy is a danger for all those in the remnant church who dare to carry out the commandments of our Lord in a bold way.

As a social worker, one of my earliest jobs was working for Children's Protective Services. While there, I was given a very strange case. I was to represent the cause of the State to remove a newborn infant from a young woman who was rumored to be a witch and who lived in the woods, having no home. I never met her or the baby, but the State won custody in court, and it was done. A few months later, for a period of several months, six dead cats showed up in my yard. I was totally and completely clueless about where they were coming from at the time. Eventually, it stopped happening, and we forgot about it.

Having never investigated witchcraft or satanism, I was not one to put these "co-incidences" together or run around pointing fingers. I was aware a little later, as an employee of the area's large Crisis Pregnancy Center and very visibly in the pro-life movement, that we received curses from the local witches; they were boldly painted in pentagrams on our building's foundation. I did not know then what enormous power they could wield as agents of the evil one. Eventually, that foundation began to shift and crumble, and our building was considered unsafe, forcing us to move into more and more expensive buildings. The cost was burdensome! As young Christians, our youth and ignorance were tempered somewhat by our elders who urged us to pray without ceasing, but we didn't truly understand what that meant for those of us in the battle for the lives of innocent babies in their mother's wombs.

Thirty Years Later:

It was another 27 years before I met a man, a former cult member himself, who told me that what I had experienced with the presence of the dead cats was a cult's or coven's blood covenant, a curse that asked blood for blood, related to the removal of that infant child. Now, it has been decisively broken off, but when I learned of this, it really broke my heart, and I could only then feel a deep, deep sorrow for those who placed me and my family under that curse. You see, by the time I learned this, I had been exposed to the awful torment and pain that those trying to leave the service of Satan endure when they turn to Jesus, having prayed with some cult members. My heart's cry for them was that I should be able to forgive them their deeds of darkness, for they knew not what they had been doing. I was already healed and made whole from the loss of my son, which had occurred in the year of the blood covenant. And I will never know if a cult really affected those circumstances to such an extent that they had anything to do with his accidental death. I do believe, however, that those who spoke those incantations or curses are likely still suffering. I did forgive them then and I continue to forgive them, in the Spirit, as Christ forgives me.

Freedom From Bondage and Oppression

All glory is given to the Father through the gift of the Holy Spirit, who created in me by His indwelling Spirit a new Identity in Christ that I never could have established for myself. This process continued for four decades! Then came an even greater transformation in me. I was led by the Spirit as He interceded for me, and Jesus spoke into me from the throne to release every chain to this earth that bound me for good or ill. I never knew what Jesus really meant about being willing to leave behind everything and everybody for the sake of the gospel until this transformation occurred. Yes, in my earliest years of zeal for the Lord, I would have left all behind. But then came the building up of my family, profession, missions, and earthly possessions. True releasing of all could not come for me until I had experienced "all" and then perceived the need to release it.

As a child of God who has been freed from extreme oppression and given the tools to stay free day after day, the last and least likely desire in my heart is to persecute anyone else in the world! I only wish the world knew this amazing grace, this love that penetrates our deepest wounds and brings healing salve.

Now, as for this man Jesus, the exact representation of my Father God, who is my King, my Lord and Savior, I can endure persecution and even go to my death!

The Persecution of the Saints Around the World

Among the many possible sources of persecution of Christians, elitist Satanists, witches, and normal everyday cult members have been accused of busily casting spells without ceasing twenty-four hours a day against Christians. However, this is not a subject that can be "googled" and researched if you wish to verify it. But if God leads you to discover more because He is giving you the burden of intercession in this area, then He will lead you off the beaten track into detailed information. I believe that you should not get involved unless God is calling you or you know that you are directly under attack and possibly need clarity about defending yourself and your loved ones.

The abundance of persecution from the Arab Shiite world is self-evident every time we turn on the news. The ayatollahs of Iran have targeted Israel, of course, as "little Satans," but the United States, the largest Christian nation in the Western world, is called the Great Satan. We now live under heightened terrorist threats almost daily. The persecution of our brothers and sisters of the Jewish nation is unrelenting and increasing as Satan continues to target the land, the home, and the family of the Lord Jesus.

The Voice of the Martyrs (VOM) website is www.per-secution.com. This is the most appropriately named website I have ever seen. A quick look will help you to understand the pervasiveness of persecution of Christ's followers today when you open the pdf. global report maps. Under the following category in the continent of Africa alone, there are eight countries:

> **Restricted** This includes countries where government-sanctioned circumstances or anti-Christian laws lead to Christians being *harassed, imprisoned, killed, or deprived of possessions or liberties because of their witness.* Also included are countries where government policy or practice prevents Christians from obtaining Bibles or other Christian literature.

There are eight nations in the Asian Pacific area surrounding China and ten countries in the Middle East. In short, the evidence of persecution is widespread.

Sadly, the nation of Israel, including the Gaza Strip and the Palestinian territory, is considered 'hostile' to Christians. The VOM defines **hostile** as:

> "…nations or large areas of nations where governments consistently attempt to provide protection for the Christian population but where Christians are routinely persecuted by family, friends, neighbors or political groups because of their witness."

Although it has not been my personal experience, I do know of Christians in Israel who must keep their witness very subdued in order to avoid government scrutiny and censorship for "evangelical" activities. Even those who are Messianic Jews must be careful in their interactions, especially with the ultra-orthodox Jews. Now that the immigration office is dominated by ultra-orthodox believers, Messianic Jews who desire to immigrate to Israel may face questioning that will screen them out and sideline their applications. Novice Christian tourists come to Israel hoping to meet and evangelize the citizens there, and routinely, they are warned sternly not to do so. It is discouraged, although not technically illegal, and can incur penalties. Some Christian missionaries have been detained and required to obtain bail, then made to pledge that they will abstain from Christian missionary activity. Many missionaries are also refused entry into the country; Christian proselytism is cited as a reason to deny student visas, work visas, and permanent residency petitions.

In the United States, we face more and more cases in which businesses, schools, and even government bureaucratic officials are challenged when their Christian values and norms put them in conflict with the prevailing post-Christian cultural norms. This is the beginning of the systematic persecution of the followers of the Way, in contrast to those outbursts of deadly persecutory violence in the church. The media, intellectual elite, and the scientific, medical, and educational communities have been almost wholly converted to the "arguments and pretension that sets itself up against the knowledge of God."[2 Cor 10:5] We are in that position now in which we are being tested and slowly immersed in the warm water that will be put on the stove one day over a high flame and will begin to boil.

How We Prepare

How does one prepare for such a time as this? Fortunately, we have a Savior who experienced the world and the buffeting of Satan and can advise us precisely how to react to persecution:

> "When they bring you before the synagogues and the rulers and the authorities, do not worry about how or what you are to speak in your defense, or what you are to say; for the Holy Spirit will

teach you in that very hour what you ought to say." [Luke 12: 11-12]

And this: "But I say to you, love your enemies and pray for those who persecute you, so that you may be sons of your Father who is in heaven." [Matt 5: 44-45]

And Paul the Apostle, who taught us:

"For though we walk in the flesh, we do not war according to the flesh, for the weapons of our warfare are not of the flesh, but divinely powerful for the destruction of fortresses. We are destroying speculations and every lofty thing raised up against the knowledge of God, and we are taking every thought captive to the obedience of Christ." [2 Cor 10: 3-5]

Dependence and Trust

Trusting Self:

I suggest we ask ourselves: on whom do we depend in this life when enemies come against us? Or in what do we place our security? Have we created our own armor, like Goliaths? Do we count on this image of ourselves encased in bronze armor with a helmet of bronze that reflects the light of our brilliance in shards to blind our enemies? Do we keep carefully hidden within that armor the truth we know about our Lord, a mind that we have renewed in Christ and yet are still timid about sharing it with the world? Is our armor a coat of scales that layers up, built over the years of our life, and interweaves tightly to defend our vital organs with cleverly devised arguments and defenses? How heavy has this coat become? Can we now move within it, or can it be pierced from without by the cries of those around us? Is our coat bound tightly to protect the wounds we bear and keep our deepest inner pain stored in the bowels of our being from spilling out in grief, longing, shame, and humiliation? This is the picture and result of trusting in and depending on oneself, even if we know who Christ is.

Trusting Jesus:

Or do we now wear the breastplate of righteousness? Christ, our righteousness, *none of it our own,* belted over with His truth, His Gospel, spoken and created in Him, who is the way, the truth, the life? And do we carry the shield of faith before us as we confront our enemies according to the gospel, loving them as we pray for those who persecute us? Is your back protected by the Father alone as all enemies fall before you and none can surround and surprise you? We need no bronze greaves around our legs like Goliath to protect us from the dogs that nip at our shins if we walk in the Gospel of Peace. Imagine the freedom and lightness with each step taken without the weight of your greaves. Father admonishes us:

> *You have a choice to make: either you create this Goliath of your own and attempt to subdue your world into submission to you, or, shedding all pretenses of your own strength, you come naked into my presence! Allow Me to equip you daily as only I can with my righteousness, My Spirit, and know my peace will fill you, My heart will beat within you, My breath will give you life and grace alone will open the door to my throne room.*

I pray that you have come to know Him intimately and completely, that Jesus' words to His disciples on that fateful night ring true in your deepest innermost spirit: "Do not let your hearts be troubled. Trust in God, trust also in me."

God Seeks Intercessors

(This brief lesson is offered with gratitude to Norman P. Grubb, the author of <u>Rees Howells, Intercessor</u>)

Pray for the persecuted church. We all need one another's prayers in these times of desperation and His peace- the Shalom that scatters the darkness, as we witness the Father's plan unfolding before our Lord brings His Kingdom!

The Call from Ezekiel:

"¹⁶ And he saw that there was no man, and wondered that there was no intercessor: therefore his arm brought salvation unto him; and his righteousness, it sustained him." Isaiah 59:16 (KJV)"

"³⁰ And I sought for a man among them, that should make up the hedge, and stand in the gap before me for the land, that I should not destroy it: but I found none." Ezekiel 22:30 (KJV)

What do we as believers think it means to be an intercessor called by God to stand in the gap, to bring the salvation of the Gospel, attest to the righteousness of God and sustain the Kingdom of God?

INTENSIFIED PRAYER: When one begins to pray intentionally to intercede for others, the amount of time that it requires will be of little concern to you. And the desire to persist in prayer will come to you often throughout the day as your spirit responds in obedience to the promptings of the Holy Spirit. Intercession will begin and end as the Father guides you, His voice speaking its completion or the need to continue often felt in the depths of one's own spirit.

Three things are necessary that are not found in ordinary prayer

- IDENTIFICATION with the pain and the conditions of those in need. Just as Jesus was fully identified with us as our Priest.
- AGONY or an emotional intensification as one identifies with the persons in need:

*"**26** Likewise the Spirit also helps in our weaknesses. For we do not know what we should pray for as we ought, but the Spirit Himself makes intercession for us[a] with groanings which cannot be uttered.* Romans 8:26

- AUTHORITY to accomplish the purposes of God.

*"**24** Most assuredly, I say to you, unless a grain of wheat falls into the ground and dies, it remains alone; but if it dies, it produces much grain/fruit."* John 12:24 (NKJV)

What allows the authority to happen in us? It's not a substitution for sin! That job has been taken and completed to perfection. First, we identify with those who are suffering over and over. Then, we come to a place where we can gain the objectives of God. As the Holy Spirit prevails in our prayers, God Hears His heart's desires being voiced in the intercessor, and God is moved!

"The weak channel is clothed with authority by the Holy Spirit and can speak the word of deliverance; Greater works are done." (Rees Howell, Intercessor)

Listening Prayers of Encouragement

On January 23, 2017, this word was revealed in listening prayer:

The shaking will reveal My glory in the testimony of my saints! For though they fear the elements, they trust in Me. Many winds must blow in this shaking, and the rains of torrential purification remove even those structures you thought were permanent. In this, the fear of nature may bear fruit of my Spirit for those who have eyes to see and ears to hear. Seek MY face and experience my Shekinah glory even now in the light of my Flowing River!

Even in darkness light dawns for the upright, for those who are gracious and compassionate and righteous.

Good will come to those who are generous and lend freely, who conduct their affairs with justice.

Surely, the righteous will never be shaken; they will be remembered forever. Ps 112:4-8

Once more I will shake not only the earth but also the heavens. The words 'once more' indicate the removing of what can be shaken- that is created things, so that what cannot be shaken may remain. Hebrews 12:26-27

They will flee to caverns in the rocks and to the overhanging crags from the fearful presence of the Lord and the splendor of his majesty, when he rises to shake the earth. Isa 2:19

The shaking is coming and must come, but He will endure forever, and we will endure IN HIM.

March 5, 2017:

Take this stylus and inscribe upon your hearts:

I AM

Your Bridegroom, Your Enforcer, Protector, Defender, a Lord who loves with unbelievable passion.

I AM HE WHO COMES.

Waste no motion or breath. Know it, see it, release it, and up the crags of a sheer wall, leap to the heights of my mountain to join my movement.

Be in ME, Be ONE as we are ONE in the Father.

Wrecked upon the shores, leave the piles of refuse, the flotsam of centuries. My waves bring refreshing beauty and clarity; nothing need be tied or fettered to another.

Shadows of evil may cloud your vision for a moment,

but the brilliance of my Son will soon scorch the ground upon which it trod.

Let there be joy in the shadows and the dancing of freedom to the flute and timbrel. Because you are anointed. The oil of wholeness flows completely finished within you and cannot but ooze forth in the pathways you walk. You are equipped for the purpose you have been called. Fear not. Do not go to Egypt!

I transcribe and share all these listening prayers from the Father through my "stylus" to you who choose to read this with joy and trepidation. A word of explanation: Egypt is where Father Abraham took his flock in their time of distress, which ended in their enslavement. I believe this is a warning to avoid being enticed by whatever the world offers as the easy way out of crushing circumstances.

We who have been listening and preparing are pressed with the urgency to share with you the absolute certainty that we can be prepared for whatever is unleashed upon us in this world at any time in the present or the future. We have read the "end of the book" and know with unshakable certainty that *we who are in Christ will bring glory to the Father!* But preparation takes time and effort in the study of the word, in fellowship with believers who challenge us to sharpen our understanding, in hours of intercessory prayer and learning the amazing 'skill', if you will, of resting in the arms of our Father, so that He speaks to us and we know His voice. The time is upon us. Begin now, if not yesterday.

Come, Lord Jesus, Come!

Reflections

1. How would you now define persecution? What is its point or purpose?
2. What does persecution look like to you in this

world, our culture, your life?

3. How have you prepared yourself: if persecution comes, how do you think you would react?
4. If you have experienced persecution, what did it look like or feel like? How did you manage it?
5. Have you been called to intercede with intensified and passionate prayer? Can you share who you were called to pray for and, if you know, how God answered? This experience really encourages the body!
6. Who do you feel needs your prayers right now?

Guidepost X

Forgiveness

The character of our Lord Jesus of Nazareth, Yeshua the Messiah, our Savior, is birthed in us through all the disciplines and experiences described in these guideposts, and yet, it is the act of forgiveness in which, I believe, we reach the greatest understanding of His sacrificial character and depth of our inadequacy. The power of the evil one is rendered impotent over us when we forgive, as Christ forgave, according to the Father's will. Healing and freedom are enlivened in us when we forgive and are forgiven. Persecution is meaningless when the persecutor is forgiven, and spiritual warfare loses its impact on us when we say "Forgive them, Lord" to those who have spoken curses over us! "Let your kingdom come *in us* as it is in Heaven"! The cry and the prayer went out from Jesus's heart and continue to echo down through the ages.

Forgiveness is evidence of God's holy new covenant given by the Spirit. It is a sacrificial, healing truth. It is righteousness that heals our suffering; it is present when He releases all His promises; it is the hope and courage to persevere in obedience. Forgiveness releases the Blessing of God and, in the end, will cause persecution to be null and void. In the face of forgiveness, persecution cannot achieve its end goal of annihilating us or our faith.

The Ministry of Reconciliation

In 2 Cor. 5:18-19, Paul writes, *"All this is from God, who reconciled us to himself through Christ and gave us the ministry of reconciliation; that God was reconciling the World to himself in Christ,* **not counting men's sins against them***."* What is 'all this' all about? We are being transformed:

Indulge me as we take a fresh look at 2 Cor 5: 13-17 but from the bottom up, starting with verse 17:

If anyone is in Christ he is a new creation[17] able to see all from God's perspective: *so from now on we regard no one from a worldly point of view* [16]; the old me has died, just as Christ died for us all. *"For Christ's love compels us, because we are convinced that one died for all, and therefore all died*[14]*"; and* now by Christ's love, I am compelled to live for Him and for others because *"he died for all, that those who live should* no longer live for themselves but for him who died for them *and was raised again*[15]*"* Now I can do "all this" and look like a crazy person to the rest of the world because *"if we are out of our minds (it is) for the sake of God* [13]*."*

Therefore, "all this" means being transformed and able to see all from God's perspective, dying to self, being compelled to live for Jesus and others, and looking crazy to the rest of the world!

But do the above scriptures mean that reconciliation is synonymous with forgiveness of sins, or is it the end result of forgiveness? The word reconciliation can mean:

1. The action of making one view or belief compatible with another, suggesting that God has changed

His mind about the consequences of my sin, or that I have changed my views to match His, or,

2. "to exchange or bring into a changed relationship."

If we are given the ministry of reconciliation[18] and know that our sins are not counted against us any longer[19] then we are living in the fruit of forgiveness, reunited with our God. I prefer this second definition as it puts the emphasis on the fruit of the changed relationship, not on who must change. Obviously, I need to change if I am in sin, but I am not able to, and if I were able to stop sinning on my own, I wouldn't need a savior! If, like Paul, I implore you, "Be reconciled to God"[20] and tell you in the same breath that Jesus took your sin so you could "become righteous,"[21] I am not splitting hairs between the act of forgiveness and the fruit of reconciliation. It is done; He has done it; now you must agree, accept it, and begin to live in that changed relationship with God!

But they are not synonymous. In fact, my daily walk determines if I am living up to or into that fullness of intimacy in my relationship with God since the forgiveness of my sin made it available to me through reconciliation. Or whether I am accumulating more boulders, stones or pebbles in my path that will block the open passage between me and my Fathers' throne room.

What is Forgiveness?

- **The Life Blood of our Savior**

Jesus said, "Father, Forgive them, for they do not know what they are doing." Luke 23:34 "And yet they knew they had "gnosis," which is Greek for intelligence or understanding and implies a surface level knowing, but not the "epignosis," which is more precise, correct or deeper knowledge, of what they did. Do any of us have total knowledge of what we do? To ourselves, to others? No, not usually. When I do reach for a deeper level of "epignosis," I become aware of the heart of the offended, and I feel, identify with, and bear their pain. *Epignosis* is full discernment. Jesus was forgiving those responsible for His crucifixion unconditionally, not depending on their coming into the full knowledge of their sin or having a change of heart first.

The Orthodox Jewish Bible uses "daas" (pronounced da-as) in this word spoken by Jesus: "They have no *daas* of what they are doing." The meaning here is no "concern, knowledge, premeditation, skill, truth or intentionality." Daas can also be translated as the "moral quality" or "knowledge" possessed by God. The highest sense of the word is "knowledge of God." In the Hebrew spelling, *Dalet-Ayin-Tav*, more is revealed: *Dalet* means a door; *Ayin* means knowing or insight; and *Tav* means a covenant sign of truth and perfection. Essentially, *daas* is entering through the door that leads to the knowledge of the covenantal truth and perfection of God.

Forgiveness is Christ's very lifeblood, the force of His life, which was spilled out to accomplish the Father's purpose in sending Him to us: the forgiveness of our sins.

• The Sovereign Way of God

"Father if you are willing take this cup from me; yet not my will but yours be done" Luke 22:42; *"Jesus commanded Peter, "Put your sword away! Shall I not drink the cup the Father has given me?"* John 18:11 And didn't He know that it was the cup of absolute forgiveness of sins, grace over all? Yes, He knew He was the sacrificial lamb born to be the final atonement for our sins.

But he has appeared once for all at the culmination of the ages to do away with sin by the sacrifice of himself. [27] Just as people are destined to die once, and after that to face judgment, [28] so Christ was sacrificed once to take away the sins of many; and he will appear a second time, not to bear sin, but to bring salvation to those who are waiting for him. [Hebrews 9: 26-28]

Therefore, when Christ came into the world, He said:

"Sacrifice and offering you did not desire, but a body you prepared for me;[6] with burnt offerings and sin offerings you were not pleased.
[7] Then I said, 'Here I am—it is written about me in the scroll— I have come to do your will, my God.'" [Hebrews 10:5-7]

Jesus, who is and was the Word made flesh, quoted the eternal word of scripture written in Psalm 40:6-8. He was about His father's business since He was a boy with self-awareness. He knew exactly what He was sent to do.

- **The Hope of Relationship with the Sovereign God, the Son, the Spirit**

Jesus answered him, "I tell you the truth, today you will be with me in paradise" [Luke 23:43]

We proclaim what we have seen and heard so that you may have fellowship with us, and our fellowship is with the Father and with His Son, Jesus Christ. We write this to make our joy complete. [5]...God is Light; in him there is no darkness at all, if we claim to have fellowship with him yet walk in darkness, we lie and do not live by the truth. But if we walk in the light, as he is in the light, we have fellowship with one another and the blood of Jesus, His Son, purifies us from all sin. [1 John 1: 3-7]

Can a person walk in the light while sin resides within? When we forgive, we remove the darkness of so many sins within ourselves, like bitterness, anger, resentment, and more, and we walk in the light. The way is opened up, as we are obedient in this area, for every other form of darkness to be removed as well.

- **The Providence (the protective spiritual care) of God in Healing**

He himself bore our sins in his body on the tree, so that we might die to sins and live for righteousness; by his wounds you have been healed. 1 Peter 2: 24

…And the power of the Lord was present for him to heal the sick…[20] When Jesus saw their faith, he said, "Friend, your sins are forgiven." (the Pharisees are questioning who can forgive sins but God alone) [22] Jesus knew what they were thinking…and asked, "Which is easier: to say 'your sins are forgiven' or to say 'Get up and walk' But that you may know the Son of man has authority on earth to forgive sins …" Jesus said to the paralyzed man. "I tell you, get up, take your mat and go home" Luke 5: 17;20,22

- **The Source of Reconciliation, Restoration and Reformation**

Jesus said to Simon Peter, "Simon, son of John, do you truly love me more than these?" "Yes, Lord", he said, "You know that I love you." Jesus said, "Feed my sheep."…" Take care of my sheep"… "Feed my sheep." John 21:15

In this act of reconciliation with Simon Peter, Jesus was reconciling with Peter, reforming his character through forgiveness and restoring his office of Apostle to His church.

If we confess our sins, he is faithful and just and will forgive us our sins and purify us from all unrighteousness. 1 John 1-9

- **The Character of Christ, His Mind, His Spirit, His Soul**

When they hurled their insults at him, he did not retaliate, when he suffered, he made no threats. Instead, he entrusted himself to him who judges justly. [1 Peter 2: 23]

But when he was a long way off, his father saw him and was filled with compassion for him; he ran to his son, threw his arms around him, and kissed him. [Luke 15:20]

The Beatitudes: [Matthew 5:1-12] Each one requires the central character trait of forgiveness, and they are the very heart, soul, and character of our Lord, breathed out for us to witness like the gentle dew on the grass of morning. His footsteps leave these traces of who He is, pressed into us. See **The Beatitudes** below.

- **The Character of Christ, His Heart; The Exact Representation of the Father**

This is **how we know what love is**: Jesus Christ laid down his life for us, and we ought to lay down our lives for our brothers. [1 John 3:16]

This is love: not that we loved God, but that he loved us and **sent his son, as an atoning sacrifice for our sins**… [1 John 4:10] And so we know and rely on the love God has for us. **God is love** and whoever lives in love, lives in God and God in him. [1 John 4:16]

In the beginning was the Word (Jesus), and the Word was with God, and the Word was God… **Through him all things were made** [John 1:1] In Him was life and **that life was the light of men.** The light shines in the darkness, but the darkness has not understood it… [John 1:4-5]

In the beginning, God created the heavens and the earth… [Genesis 1:1] So **God created man in His own image.** [Genesis 1:27]

I don't think I can express the truth any more clearly than the above Scriptures: that Love is forgiveness of sin, God is Love, and the Word is Jesus. Our Savior, the Son of Man, is one with God, and He created by His Word the life of men, from the beginning of creation, all made in the image of the Word, Jesus, and through the Love of God. Further words fail this mortal writer. The experience of being personally restored through forgiveness, then of seeing lives restored in the healing and prayer ministry through forgiveness, and the radical transformation of minds, emotions, and character that occurs is the best witness to this incredible truth.

- **The Glue that holds the Universe in Place**

"If those days had not been cut short, no one would survive, but for the sake of the elect, those days will be shortened." Matthew 14:22

The elect are those who have been chosen, <u>forgiven</u>, and reconciled to God.

"The Lord is angry with all the nations… he will totally destroy them…All the stars of the Heavens will be dissolved, and the sky rolled up like a scroll; all the starry host will fall." Isaiah 34: 2,4 However, remember that "The desert and the parched land will be glad; the wilderness will rejoice and blossom. Isaiah 35:1 …But only the <u>redeemed</u> will walk there. And the <u>ransomed</u> of the Lord will return, they will enter Zion with singing." Isaiah 35:9-10

Does it make sense to you, as it does to me, that without His decision and ability to forgive us, the whole universe would simply blow apart and cease to exist! He has created a universe as a place for the elect who are reconciled, redeemed, and ransomed to walk in, to return to, to enter with singing. We, who have been <u>forgiven,</u> are the reason for all of this to go on.

- **The Reason for sin and evil and separation from God to exist**

As they led Him away, they laid hold of a certain man, Simon…
and on him, they laid the cross that he might bear it after Jesus.
Luke 23: 26

First, look at this moment of greatest darkness; evil
was temporarily rejoicing, and this man was drawn into
that dark moment. What do you think he gained in the
days and years following that awful assignment to bear
Jesus' cross for Him? Which one of these following truths
do you think that Simon learned first if he became a
follower of the Way after this?

"I want to know Christ—yes, to know the power of his resurrection and participation in his sufferings, becoming like him
in his death, [11] and so, somehow, attaining to the resurrection
from the dead" Phil 3:10-11

"I have been crucified with Christ and I no longer live, but Christ
lives in me. The life I now live in the body, I live by faith in the
Son of God, who loved me and gave himself for me" Galatians 2:20

But I tell you, love your enemies and pray for those who persecute you, [45]that you may be children of your Father in heaven.
He causes his sun to rise on the evil and the good, and sends
rain on the righteous and the unrighteous. Matthew 5:44

But this happened so that the works of God might be displayed
in him. John 9:3

I don't know the end of Simon's story. No one does.
However, if the Father chose him for the task of carrying
our Lord's cross, he must have had more reason than most
to desire to know this Christ, to identify with His life and
death, His suffering and resurrection, and the power of

forgiveness that caused Jesus to utter those famous last words: "Father, forgive them for they know not what they do." Did Simon carry some of the guilt for his participation in that crucifixion by carrying the instrument of our Lord's torture? We are not told any of his thoughts or feelings. I imagine that in order for him to live out his days with himself, he must have sought out all these truths, and especially the depth of meaning that is forgiveness for the evil act he was forced to participate in.

If then, forgiveness did not exist in God's mind from the beginning, He, who desires our reconciliation with Him above all things because of His amazing love, would likely not have allowed evil to exist, to have tried us all with temptations and suffering, and to have tested us to the point where we turn to Him in utter surrender and beg for His forgiveness and reconciliation.

The Beatitudes

How Can We Walk in the Forgiving Character of Christ?

Nothing like forgiveness identifies us so completely with the person, the passion, and the purpose of Christ. This absolute, cornerstone principle of forgiveness is so intrinsic to Jesus that in the entire sermon that we call the Beatitudes, He doesn't even mention the word *forgiveness*. However, as we examine each Beatitude, it becomes apparent that it is a key ingredient, although not necessarily the only ingredient, in every quality or personal characteristic He mentions.

Blessed are the poor in spirit, for theirs is the kingdom of heaven (Matt 5:3).

If you ask yourself how to attain this degree of humility, your answer must include letting go of all personal pride and desire for worldly success <u>and</u> forgiving all your enemies, turning the other cheek to insult or injury, perhaps relinquishing all your money or possessions to a stranger on the road, and more. It requires you to daily and actively forgive every offense. And "God opposes the proud but gives grace to the humble." ^{James 4:6} Only in humility do we recognize our sinfulness and the need for our savior's redemptive forgiveness.

Blessed are those who mourn, for they will be comforted (Matt 5:4).

How and when does the Comforter come? He comes quickly when natural death claims a loved one, but when I lose someone in difficult, painful ways—disease, accident, divorce, abandonment, war, and any number of tragedies—then I will grieve and be flooded with other emotions. Anger, bitterness, confusion, despair, and hopelessness take over my soul, and the comforter cannot comfort me, not until I forgive.

Any source of painful loss in this world, *even* the worst imaginable, must be forgiven in and out of our obedience to God, who is also our Lord. When we understand that all who do *evil* things are under the power and authority of the rulers of the air and unable to understand the things of God, the problem of the ultimate judgment for evil and rectifying wrongs is eventually released and given over to God.

When I am obedient, the Holy Spirit, my Comforter, will come and bring light to my darkest night. In this holy transaction of forgiveness, done in faith and obedience, when I offer forgiveness, God responds with a miraculous healing of my heart, lifting the burden from me and yoking me to Him with His love. This level of forgiveness may not be humanly possible, but in Christ, and the power of the Holy Spirit, it is possible.

Blessed are the meek, for they will inherit the earth (Matt 5:5).

The meek and the humble share many of the same characteristics: letting go of all worldliness and pride and forgiving all insults and injuries. Yet, Jesus singles out the meek for a special inheritance. Are the meek perhaps those of us who never presumed or sought after a higher status, position, power, education, or influence? They could be described almost as "humble from birth." The dictionary defines meek as "having or showing a quiet and gentle nature: not wanting to fight or argue with other people (submissive, yielding, obedient, deferential)." But how did they come by such a wise and gentle, submissive spirit so completely that their lives are wholly devoted to God?

No matter what was fed into their lives in the way of Godly parents or wholesome teaching and training to walk upright before God, they became meek *when they forgave others*: the bullies on the bus, the kids who never wanted them around, the tired parent who yelled at them, the coach who overlooked them, the boss who gave someone else the raise. The meek in Christ, however, never feel like doormats because they know whom they submit to!

Forgiveness and meekness, humility, and the comfort of the Comforter combine in those individuals of whom Jesus says:

Blessed are those who hunger and thirst for righteousness, for they will be filled (Matt 5:6).

How beautifully the Lord patiently teaches us and draws us to Him when we are yearning to follow His ways! Does your soul yet "yearn and cry out, even faint for the courts of the living God"? [Ps 84:1-2] Jesus promises that you will be filled! But if there is bitterness, anger, and unforgiveness within you, it will war against the hunger you feel for righteousness, because the two cannot co-exist forever.

Blessed are the merciful, for they will be shown mercy (Matt 5:7).

The merciful cannot be merciful unless they forgive the offender. Our theology describes mercy as compassion, pity, and the patience of God. But if forgiveness is shown toward someone whom it is within one's power to punish or harm, then mercy has been shown. It is the essence of the compassionate act of mercy. Before the foundations of the earth and for all time, the act of mercy, God's free gift of grace (an undeserved gift of forgiveness) hangs on the cross; for all time, the symbol of man's reconciliation to God through Christ's sacrifice. The cross is the symbol of that sacrifice and of redemption through forgiveness.

Blessed are the pure in heart, for they will see God (Matt 5:8).

Can an individual ever become pure in heart without giving and receiving the gift of forgiveness? And can anything other than forgiveness ultimately allow us to "see God"? So here is the challenge, the gauntlet thrown down, your deepest desire: to see God! It is not out of reach. That purity **can** come as we "put out the trash," as one friend says. Daily forgive; daily confess and receive forgiveness; forgive ourselves and God as well, because He longs for us to be His pure and blameless bride, without stain or wrinkle or any other blemish (Eph 5:27), as we enter His courts.

Blessed are the peacemakers, for they will be called sons of God (Matt 5:9).

Jesus, the Son of God, came to be the ultimate peacemaker, reconciling us all to God through forgiveness, gracefully and freely given to us through His Love, which *is* active forgiveness.

I want to be a Peacemaker, a child of God. So, as my teacher, Erin, says, "The first rule of engagement is "DO NOT ENGAGE." Let go of the rope when you are in the midst of strife with another. They will fall, but as you are left standing, you can forgive them and offer them a helping hand again, bringing restoration and peace. If you are the one to fail like Simon Peter, whom Jesus admonished to strengthen his brothers when he had turned back, Luke 22:31 would you be able to re-enter that ministry to which Jesus called you unless you received His forgiveness, forgave yourself, and received forgiveness from your fellow disciples?

> Blessed are those who are persecuted because of righteousness, for theirs is the kingdom of heaven ... and you when people insult you, persecute you and say all kinds of evil against you because of my name, rejoice and be glad for great is your reward in heaven. Matt 5: 10-12

Jesus wanted to deliver this final ultimate message and challenge to us, but He carefully and lovingly prepared the ground beforehand, delivering the promises of God with each quality and trait of character that He would work into our souls and spirit. All we have to do is cooperate with Him as we seek righteousness and forgive every step of the way. When that is done, those who have been obedient, have trusted and sought Him in faith, and believed in His promises will understand that they can forgive those who persecute them as well. In fact, they will long to do so for Christ Jesus' sake. The compassion of Christ may work in the mind of the one being persecuted to know that the act of forgiveness right here and now, as he perhaps faces death, could be the catalyst that will save yet another soul for Christ. The knowledge of the power of forgiveness will be so deep within us, knowing that "nothing can separate us from the love of God which is in Christ Jesus," that no word or action against us will shatter our oneness and our union with Him in this life and in His dwelling place for eternity.

Forgiveness Changes Everything

The experience of receiving or giving forgiveness can be absolutely supernatural in its intensity and in the instantaneous change it works into the seeker. When it is given in the presence and power of the Holy Spirit, it seems to transform the giver's emotional state so completely that they truly have a new character. This is most apparent when forgiveness is given in obedience to the Lord, especially when the "natural" man doesn't feel like forgiving and cannot imagine ever reconciling with whoever or whatever has hurt them. Obedience allows the power of God to act, regardless of our emotional state or our beliefs about what is right or wrong, and in that act, we invite Him in to change us. This obedience does not require that we are even considering reconciliation. Soon, however, the fruit of the Spirit begins to grow in us: love, joy, peace, patience, kindness, goodness, faithfulness, gentleness, and self-control. Gal 5: 22-23 Reconciliation may follow or may not. But it can begin when forgiveness opens the door.

A Testimony of Forgiveness

I shared earlier how difficult it was for my marriage when Blair died, partially because the integrity of my husband's faith was sorely compromised with doubts about God; how could he trust a God who allowed the accident to occur, and regain respect for me? As is natural in man, who seeks to understand cause and effect in order to protect his family and himself, he thought I had allowed the accident to happen. In the almost 30 years since then, we have traveled the road towards divorce and back again, over the terrain of separation and despair, to forgiveness and reconciliation several times.

Each time was necessary for our relationship to grow in depth and understanding and for the truth of the gospel to be glorified. The last time occurred several years ago, when I made the choice to go to a conference over our anniversary, thinking I had explained that fact adequately, and made arrangements to celebrate when I returned. My husband didn't see it that way. In fact, he was very hurt and jealous! But what came out of his mouth were words so hurtful that character assassination barely describes it. It was more like the assassination of our marriage, and the entire meaning of our relationship was denigrated to the lowest level I'd ever imagined possible. I was outraged and told him to leave and never return. It was over, and I was through! I was finished with trying and never wanted to see him again. That was how deeply I was cut. He did leave that evening, and I left for my 3-day conference.

Fortunately, it was a very deep and moving spiritual-renewal conference! I believe God had that planned out for me ahead of time. But even so, imagine my surprise when Abba Daddy woke me up at 5 am and said, "Call him, forgive him, and tell him to come home." My reaction was outrage: "No way, God, you must be out of your mind! Didn't you hear what he said to me?!!! It didn't take me long to realize that absolute obedience to the Father was not optional, and I didn't want to go down the route of disobedience just to take a stand and sit in my anger, bitterness, resentment, deep pain, and rejection, in addition to the word curse that had been laid upon me. Defiance towards God was not the mountain I was willing to die on! I knew there was something better than this.

I made the call. At 5:15 a.m., my husband had stopped riding, parked his motorcycle, and gone into a restaurant somewhere deep in the Appalachian foothills. I was somewhat surprised that he answered the phone, as I had hoped I'd get off with leaving a message. That's not the way that Father chose to work this one out. I said the words, "I forgive you," in obedience, and he responded, came home, and the marriage counseling began soon after. I can only testify that today, we have a much deeper love and respect for one another, as well as a better understanding of our differences as individuals and the needs we each have to live out our lives as fully and fruitfully as possible. We will always be very different in the way we walk out our faith and live our lives, but that's OK, and it's the Lord's plan as well. Iron sharpens iron, and we two strong-willed individuals need the fire and flame of a very hot forge to pound out the kinks in our armor, it seems.

Listening Prayer, Thursday, August 31, 2017

Totality; the eclipse of the sun (the Son) by the moon created darkness that was completed in the path of totality. This sign to you says, "Behold how the totality of the plans and purposes of the evil one creates a pathway that encircles the earth in darkness. It is temporary, and the next revolution hides the moon again. Back in its place, you feel no threat of darkness. It seems to emit light, but that is only the reflection of my Son (sun). Signs and wonders, scientific and precise, are credible to all, yet truly seen by few: totality says 'caution, you have a zone - a period of time – and one revolution will complete it.

Completion will come. It is inevitable. It is the Steeple Point that pierces the Veil when every turning has turned and advanced into the Heart of Me in order for Me to pierce and pour out completion upon My created order. You understand the ministry of reconciliation.

This is the completion of every revolution. It begins as the blood flows fresh to purify the wounds of my people, and it doesn't stop until my entire Heart is opened up and the created is one again within Me, the Creator.

Again, I say, do not stop the flow. Allow impurities to bleed out. It must be so. Forgiveness is the flow of my blood into reconciliation.

Your Key for the Journey: Forgiveness is the lifeblood of our Savior, the flow of our salvation.

Forgiveness is key to all the steps and guideposts as we move up towards Jerusalem, and in God's timing, although we are continuously in the process of maturing, or sanctification, we are continuously able to walk in total forgiveness for our failures. This is a great and wonderful paradox of the most High Holy One who wants us to attain righteousness to be in and with Him, so much so that He gives us His very own righteousness! 2 Cor 5:21

Reflections

1. How many qualities and characteristics of the Lord reflect forgiveness?
2. Have you experienced the life-giving death of oneself through the act of forgiveness? If so, make a record of it here and now, never to be forgotten, but rather shared liberally.
3. If there is a major debtor yet to be forgiven in your life, do not fear the process. Remember that forgiveness is not equal to reconnection into a relationship. It may or may not open that door. But it will remove the burden in your heart. Make your plan now. What will you do first?
4. As you look over the beatitudes, is there one in

particular you would like to see more of in your life? Does it require forgiveness of someone?

5. What must you do to be one of the pure in heart who will see God?

6. Why do you think Yeshua said from the cross, "Forgive them, Lord, for they know not what they do"?

7. How many times must we put Him back up on that cross before we learn His ultimate lesson? And yet *We Are Forgiven!*

Final Key for the Journey

Whatever God put in us through the trials and temptations, the high mountains and valleys of our life, reflects His specific pure purpose for us each. We have an individual identity that we must submit to Christ, and He will *redeem it* and **use it,** or **we will lose it** through His healing, transformative hands.

I sincerely desire to end this book with a Word of Truth from my Abba-Father, and this is what He clearly spoke this morning:

Our God has within His mind an Infinite place of Creation, and it is a matrix where time ceases and healing is birthed! In His mind, all truth rests—that of physics, that of science—of genetics and neurobiology. That of relationships. Where wholeness and health in the human mind, body, soul and spirit, begin and end, as they continue, inside that creation matrix, all other brokenness created by Satan's interference –Ends.

God alone can Draw His beloved creatures into this Matrix and In the Presence where He Always Exists, remove the stain of the past.

This is why, beloved, when you pray in Yeshua's powerful name, and you have entered into that existence, the need you speak is met by our loving Father! The layers of pain, rejection, abandonment, and abuse are removed, and the very essence of the Body, Soul, and Mind is returned to us Purified. Somehow, He also removes the pain of memories of all the sick reactions you have entered into as you tried to deal with pain—addictions, broken relationships—and they are healed. The grip they had on the present No Longer Exists in Him, in His Creation Matrix.

Never cease praying for yourself and others. Speak and direct my Spirit Mind towards the enemy, and I will indeed Set You Free, again and again as John spoke it so long ago:

If I, the Son, set you free, you will be FREE indeed.

John 8:36

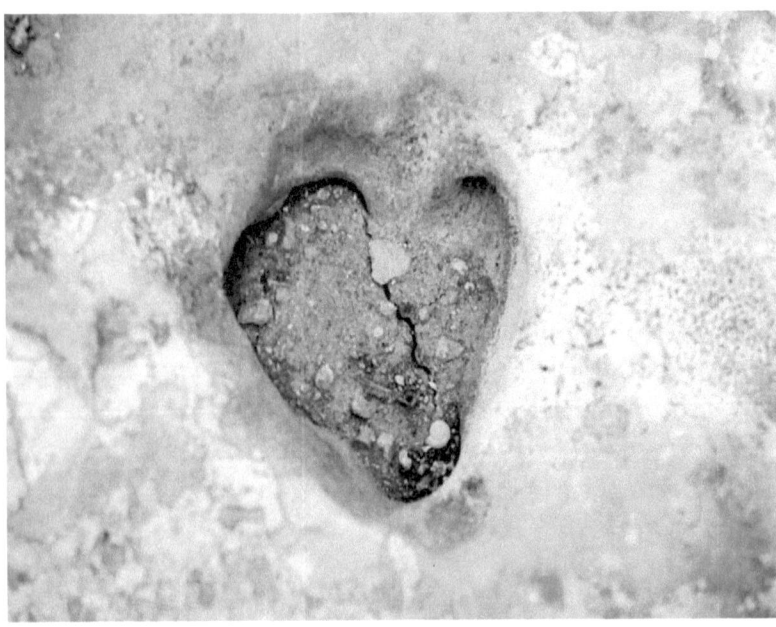

This photo of a heart shape formed in rock was taken at Shiloh, the site of the Tabernacle for 300+ years. It's really there. It looked to all of us on this journey that God's heart was breaking, and He meant for us to be aware of how tenuous things are at this time on the earth.

Conclusion

This is a story and book born of a lifetime of experiences that include deep pain, loss, and sorrow but even deeper healing and profound joy because of the greatest Love the world has ever known: Jesus Christ, my Savior and Lord, who I pray is now your Lord and Savior if He wasn't before.

The writing of this book began through the inspiration of the Holy Spirit while I was in Israel some years ago. The completion of it has blessed me and taught me immeasurably! I have been honored to hold the stylus as He dictated so much of what has been shared here.

What I have learned or what I have taught—none of my life really—would have been humanly possible without Jesus. Although I may seem like a pretty average, old retiree living a life of ease in the country, this is just the surface reality. Who I am is quietly grateful and always mindful of the brokenness and the wealth of experience my Savior has granted me. And I am always ready to counsel or mentor the pilgrims Father points in my direction, so that I can now give Him in return the Glory and Hallelujah for His magnificent salvation, continuous forgiveness, and healing! All to the Lord most High, my Father, my Friend, my ever-present Holy Spirit.

In His Love,

Elaine